THE LAST
CONCERT

by

Maynard Turow

Dedication

This book is dedicated to my father,
Israel Stanley Turow.

May he be remembered for his beautiful music,
insatiable love of the violin and immense courage in
his lust for life...

Disclaimer

This book is based on actual events as remembered by family in the life of Israel Stanley Turow. Some names, places and events have been changed at the discretion of the author to accommodate date and storyline. Any similarity to persons or places living or dead is strictly coincidental.

COPYRIGHT © 2022
Maynard Turow

ISBN 9798837313325

Table of Contents

INTRODUCTION

When Mottell Turowofsky, Israel's grandfather died, he left his hand-made Stradivarius violin to Israel's father, Izik. But Izik had no interest in the violin as he was too busy earning a living. There was no time for anything else.

The violin was kept in a hall closet to gather dust. One day, while playing in the house, Israel came upon the strange black case. The youngster had no idea at the time that this strange case and its contents would be the thread so tightly woven throughout his life, that would bring so much success, joy, and happiness. And at the end, sadness.

Israel opened up the case and touched the violin and bow. It seemed so strange and yet so beautiful. He put it away and later told his mother what he had found. She smiled and said, "It's for you. Maybe one day, when you get older, you'll learn to play it." From that day on, Israel Stanley Turowofsky played with his new toy. He would try to play the instrument, not having any idea of what he was doing, creating the most horrible sounds. But after a few months, Israel started to learn that by moving the fingers of his left hand to different positions on the violin's neck and strings, he would make much prettier sounds. Each month, the sounds got better and better, until he realized he could play some very simple melodies. One day, when his mother heard him play, she realized his potential and knew it was time for a professional teacher. Somehow, someway, she would find the extra money for his lessons. Israel Turowofsky took his first violin lesson at age five.

Israel Turow — his last name changed when he arrived at Ellis Island — became an outstanding musician, playing piano, banjo, guitar, and other instruments as well. He also led his own orchestra. But his real pleasure came from the one instrument that had captured his heart at the early age of five in Russia — the violin.

After arriving in America at age eight, the violin continued to be his pride and joy. Playing and studying music from childhood through adulthood, he became a violin virtuoso. His popularity grew in New York and Baltimore, receiving many featured articles. A *Baltimore Sun* newspaper article once called him a "musical genius". He won many awards, including scholarships to The Peabody Institute in Baltimore and the Juilliard School of Music in New York. However, his crown jewel, most cherished achievement, was the opportunity to be the featured soloist with the New York Symphonic Orchestra in Carnegie Hall. Unfortunately, the dreaded disease would not leave him. Could he fight it? Would he have enough strength for one more concert?

This is his story...

PROLOGUE

It was a stormy night outside the tiny synagogue on Barkly Street, just across from Mom and Dad's confectionary store. The men were standing, chanting a prayer. Uncle Herman held my hand. As I looked up, the men seemed so tall, like statues going right to the ceiling. Uncle Herman was sobbing into a handkerchief. I knew something terrible had happened to Daddy. Just a few days ago, Mom had sat me down to tell me, "Your Daddy has gone to heaven." She held me close. I started to cry, I was confused.

Was he ever coming back? I didn't think people ever came back once they went to heaven.

Just last week, Uncle Leonard drove Mom and me to Johns Hopkins Hospital to see Daddy. He had been there a few days and I really missed him. When we arrived inside the large dark halls of the hospital's lobby, the first thing I noticed in front of me was a very large statue of a lady. She had a shawl over her head as she looked down. It was the largest statue I had ever seen. I stopped for a moment to look up at her. In the dim light of the hospital, I was frightened. Mom gently grabbed my hand, pulling me along as I kept looking back at the large lady.

After a long walk through many halls, we finally came to an open room that much brighter. There was a large wooden desk with a nurse seated behind it. I couldn't hear what the nurse was saying to Mom and Uncle Leonard. Finally, Mom bent down and said to me, "Dear, they won't let children under twelve years old in the hospital." I was only seven and I started to cry. Uncle Leonard looked down at me and said, "It's okay because you can see your Daddy on his balcony from the back courtyard." The nurse said, "It will be fine — all the children do it!" My first thought was — I guess there's a lot of kids back there!

Uncle Leonard and I walked away as Mom threw me a kiss. We walked outside and around the entire building before we came to a grassy courtyard in the back with many benches. To my surprise, there were no children. I wasn't sure where Daddy was. Uncle Leonard looked around and then up. Then he said to me, "There he is, way up there!" I looked up, further and further, as far as I could. The sun was in my eyes and I couldn't see a thing. With my right hand I blocked the sun and finally saw him... the familiar sight of Daddy's brown and red flannel robe, the one I cuddled in so often when he held me. There he was, waving to me and giving me that wonderful smile. I waved back. Then I heard his voice. "Have you been a good boy?" I yelled back, "Yes, like I promised." He waved again and then turned to Mommy. I think he had to sit down. Mommy led him away from the balcony. That was the last time I saw my father.

The men were still praying. Uncle Herman bent down, handing me the book and said, "Try to read with us!" He knew I had been going to the Hebrew School upstairs for two years. I could read a little. "Yis Kadal Va Yis Kadal Schmi Ri Ba..."

CHAPTER 1

For twenty four days since leaving the pier at Longnoff 21, Okhotsk, Russia, the ship heaved, hoed, and yawed through the never-ending murky ocean water. Israel was leaving Russia to go to America with his mother Jenny, sisters Ida and Sadi, and little brother Herman. His older brother Morris and father Izik had left three months before, when they were promised jobs at the Baltimore Clothing Factory by Uncle Sam. His older sister Sophie had left for America a year ago and was living in New York. Izik said he would bring the whole family over as soon as he got settled and saved some money.

Finally, after three months of very little mail, the important letter came from Father. "All is good. We're living with Uncle Sam in Baltimore and there's plenty of room for the whole family. I'm enclosing passenger tickets and extra cash in the form of Money Orders. Let me know when you're coming. Love Izik." Jenny put the letter down, excited and dazed for the moment, she started to cry. She then yelled as loud as she could, running throughout the house to the children, "We're going to America!" All the children ran to her, not sure what she had said. They had all heard the word "America!"

It took days for the family to harness their excitement and get ready for the trip. The next ship to Ellis Island, New York City, United States of America, was the *Noranikoff*, scheduled to sail in two weeks. There was so much to do! Each day was another chore of packing something and saying goodbye to friends and distant relatives. Israel was excited but nervous about how he would be carrying his pride and joy, his violin. No matter what Israel packed, he kept his eye on his violin and case. He didn't want it misplaced or even touched by anyone else. Even though he tried to practice every day, his heart wasn't in it. He could hear the difference in his music, his thoughts were somewhere far away in a distant land called America. The family counted the hours as the fourteen days seemed to go on forever.

Finally, the departure date arrived and they were on their way.

The ship was about as long as a soccer field. It seemed forever to get from bow to stern. First class passengers lived above on decks four through eight. The economy passengers, like the Turowofskys, were down below on decks one, two, and three. Economy passengers could lounge on their own outside decks or go to the front of the ship to relax in the fresh air. Deck chairs were scattered all around but were quickly taken. The First class passengers sat around on the sides of the ship in plush reserved deck chairs. Often, the economy passengers could hear live music coming from the stern of the ship where first class were being entertained. Meals were taken in the large economy dining hall on the lower deck. Living quarters were a series of large rooms with wood and canvas cots for sleeping.

Generally, each room slept six to ten people. Families stayed close together, sharing as needed. The bathrooms were down the hall, about thirty feet away. In contrast, the first class cabins came complete with living room, bedroom, and bathroom. Some even had outside balconies. None of this mattered, the Turowofskys were on their way to the United States of America. They were thrilled!

CHAPTER 2

The third day at sea, Israel started to feel sick to his stomach. He couldn't eat much and stayed on his cot most of the day. When bedtime came, he hardly slept. What bothered him the most was not being able to practice the violin, which he usually did for at least two hours, or longer, every day. But he couldn't now, he was too sick to even try. His mother was told by the ship's doctor that he had a typical case of sea sickness and with some medication should be better soon. After a few days, just as he was advised, Israel started to feel close to normal.

On a beautiful warm sunny day, he decided to go outside and sit on the deck chair and read. The sea air had a clean, fresh smell and he was so happy to be feeling better. He decided, if he could eat lunch, then later in the afternoon he would try to practice his violin. While sitting and relaxing, he could hear the faint sound of music playing and wondered where it was coming from. From the corner of his eye, he noticed two boys walking along the deck. He wondered where the other kids were because when boarding, there were dozens of them. As the boys passed him, he pretended to be reading and not noticing them. However, he was thinking how great it would be to meet some new friends on the ship instead of the stuffy old-timers he kept bumping into. He wasn't sure why he hid his face in the book, instead of trying to be friendly. Why am I so shy, he wondered. As the two boys passed him, for a quick moment they glanced down at him, then quickly looked away, continuing to walk without saying a word.

On second thought, Israel was damn sorry he hadn't said something as they passed. A few seconds later, Israel looked up and saw one boy heading his way. This time, he was going to keep his head up and try to be cordial. In a fleeting moment, there in the sunlight was this tall, well-built stranger looking down at him, extending his hand saying, "Hi, I'm Arnold Hartmanoff!"

Israel shook his hand, answering, "Hello, I'm Israel Turowofsky!" Israel was beaming, thrilled to meet a new kid.

The stranger said, "My friends call me Arnie." Israel replied, "Everyone calls me Israel."

"No nickname, huh?"

"None that I know of," replied Israel." "Where are you from?" questioned Arnie. "The Lebetz area of

Yakutsk."

Arnie shot back, "Hey, that's not too far from my home in Connez, about 400 kilometers!"

Israel answered, "I've heard of it but never been there, too far to walk."

"The guy I was walking with, Sigmond Rushoff, is from Kiev. He works down in the kitchen during the voyage to help pay for the trip."

"Damn good idea," said Israel, as he climbed out of the deck lounge and stood next to Hartmanoff. Israel came up to his shoulders. Arnie was a stocky, well-built lad, looking much older than Israel. Israel had always been on the thin side, average height. As he sized up his buddy he finally asked, "I'm eight, how old are you, Arnie?"

"I'm ten and a half," he shot back.

The younger boy thought even being only two and a half years older, Arnie was a big kid! Finally, Hartmanoff belted out, "Want to take a walk around the deck and see what's going on? I can hear music in the background, wonder where it's coming from."

"I'd like to," answered Israel, "but I've got some studying to do down below." Israel didn't want to tell him about the violin right now, guessing the boy might think him a little on the sissy side because he played a musical instrument.

"Well, nice meeting you, see you around," Arnie said as he darted off.

"Yea, see you around," replied Israel, as he started to sit back down. He again realized, he was sorry he didn't walk with the guys. He really wanted to make new friends. But what the hell, his music came first! He headed down below to practice his violin.

CHAPTER 3

A few days later, while reading on the deck, out of the blue Arnie appeared. "Hi," he called.

"Hi yourself," Israel answered.

"Hey look, do you mind if I call you Izzy? Israel's too hard to remember,"Arnie said.

Israel smiled and thought out loud, "I've never had a nickname before, sure it's okay with me."

"Done," said Arnie as he shook Israel's hand. "Let's go for a walk, get you off your buns!" This time Israel jumped up without even thinking about it. The two strolled off.

Almost every day the boys would meet for their usual walk around the deck, often stopping to greet people along the way. Still, not many kids. They talked about everything, their families, their lives back home but mostly about the wonderful times they were planning to have in their new country. But one thing Israel did not talk about was the violin. For some reason, he held back speaking about his pride and joy. Arnie loved sports, constantly speaking about his favorite football heroes and looking forward to playing games with American kids. Israel mostly listened. His spare time was different, he was devoted to music, every day at 2 pm. Sometimes, when practicing back in Russia, he would peek out the living room window and see many of his friends playing in the street. Occasionally, they would peek in and watch him. Many times his mother asked, "Do you want to take a break and go out and play?" Israel would reply, "Not now, maybe later!" Rarely did the violin player leave his music and go play outside.

When he did, he made sure his lesson for the day was finished, if not he practiced again in the evening.

Arnie blurted out, "What do you do after school, in your spare time, any hobbies?"

Israel hesitated, then answered, "I read a lot and sometimes help my folks around the house."

Arnie shot back, "I don't get it! You gotta do something in your spare time! I'm always playing some kind of ball when I get a chance. I love American football, they even have a touch game that kids play... can't wait to try it in the new country!"

After hearing Arnie speak, Israel thought back on rare occasions when he enjoyed throwing and catching a ball. But he had to be careful not to hurt his hands.

15

He knew his fingers and hands had to be perfect to play his instrument. Once he hurt his fingers catching a ball and swore he wouldn't let that happen again.

Almost every day you could find Israel, Arnie, and sometimes other boys hanging around the deck telling stories or funny jokes and laughing as boys do. Often, they would tease the girls who would occasionally pass by. But, at two pm sharp, Israel left the boys to go below to practice his favorite instrument. He always made up a different excuse to get away.

CHAPTER 4

One day while strolling the decks, Izzy and Arnie were curious about the music they continued to hear. They knew it was live music and had to be coming from somewhere in first class. It had such a beautiful sound! They decided to walk as far as they could to the edge of the fantail where economy met first class on the starboard side. The two classes were separated by stairs and a large swinging picket gate with a purser, dressed in white, standing by. The gate opened and closed for first class coming and going as they showed their IDs to the guard. At a moment, when no passengers were passing by, the boys put their faces on the gate, gawking at the sight of first class eloquently dressed, mostly in white, dining and dancing and having such a wonderful time. The boys were caught by surprise with mouths wide open as the purser came up and asked, "Are you coming through or not?"

They hesitated for a moment, then Arnie spoke up. "We left our IDs in our room, can we bring them tomorrow?"

"Well, be sure you do, I'll be here!" said the man in

white.

The boys quickly hurried through the gate and kept walking as though they had a destination. As they strolled down first class, their hearts were beating a mile a minute. There in the distance, at the end of the fantail they could see the orchestra. As they got closer, the beautiful music became louder and louder. They could clearly see the stately sight of the musicians, dressed up in their military white pants, shirts, bowties, and shoes with short scarlet jackets and matching caps. They looked like toy soldiers from a story book. There, about ten feet from the musicians, was a small empty table with four chairs. Without saying a word, Arnie pointed, and they both headed for the empty seats. They slipped into the chairs as if they really belonged and looked casually around.

Neither said a word. Izzy targeted the violin players, mesmerized by their familiar sound. Surprisingly, Arnie also focused on the musicians, as they played a series of waltzes. The orchestra consisted of six violins, three violas, one cello, an English horn, and three flutes. After a few minutes, Arnie leaned in on the table with his elbows, rested his chin in his hands and muttered, "It must be wonderful to be gifted and make music like that. I really envy singers and musicians. I love music, I just never had the time or money to get involved!"

Without taking his eyes off the orchestra, Israel answered softly, "I play the violin."

Arnie turned and asked, "What did you say?"

Israel repeated, this time a little louder, "I play the violin."

"You're kidding, aren't you, you're bullshitting me, right? I mean, you're only eight now, when in the hell did you start?"

"When I was five", the younger boy answered.

For a second, Arnie laughed, then looked at Izzy, pointing and saying, "That's what you do at two pm every day, isn't it?"

"That's right, I didn't want to say anything... I thought you'd think I was a sissy or something when I didn't want to play ball," explained Israel. "Well, I'll be damned. Sissy? Hell, I think it's great, just can't believe you started at five! Hey, Izzy, can I hear you play sometime?" asked Arnie. "Sure, anytime I practice you're welcome to join. Often, several neighbors near our quarters come to watch while I'm playing."

"I'll be there today at two, for sure Izzy! Holy shit, I can't believe this!" barked Arnie.

The boys nodded in agreement and then went back to watching and listening to the orchestra. Arnie kept turning his head to the musicians, then back to Israel in amazement, while repeating, "I don't believe this... I just don't believe this!" After about ten minutes, the boys decided they were hungry and decided to go down below for lunch. They headed back off the fantail towards the stairway leading down to the gate entering economy. Near the stairs was a large sign:

TALENT SHOW SATURDAY NIGHT! INTERESTED GUESTS COME TO TRYOUT IN SOCIAL HALL MONDAY AND TUESDAY AT 10 AM. ALL SINGERS AND DANCERS WELCOME!

CHAPTER 5

Arnie asked, "Hey Izzy, why don't you give it a try?"

"It didn't say anything about playing an instrument and besides, I'm in economy. I'm sure it's only for first class," answered Izzy.

"Well, it's up to you, come on, I'm starved!" yelled Arnie. The boys headed down below. After lunch, the usual sitting around on the deck took place. The gang kept repeating the same boring stories, which became monotonous after a while. Everyone knew being confined to a ship on a journey with no stops made the days drag. But Israel, being the youngest, tried to be attentive and laugh at the jokes. He also kept looking at his watch. At two pm sharp, he said his usual, "See ya later" to the boys and headed inside.

"Hey, wait up," hollered Arnie, "I've got to help you move that bed!" Puzzled, Israel looked at him, then noticed the wink in Arnie's eye. "Oh yea, thanks," was the answer. Together, both boys headed inside. There was light chatter from some neighbors and family that gathered, as Israel and Arnie entered the quarters. Israel introduced his friend, who got a warm welcome from Mother. Everything went silent the moment Israel reached in the corner for his violin case. Opening it, out came a beautiful shiny wood-grained instrument, which was meticulously guided under Israel's chin. Arnie watched with amazement as this eight year old got everyone's attention. He noticed the careful placement of the right hand holding the bow, graceful yet strong, starting to touch the strings. Jenny was beaming and yet worried, knowing this was the first time her son would be playing for an audience and hoping it would not bother him. It didn't! Israel was cool and collected as he started a slow warm-up, hitting each string and then matching scales up and down several octaves.

Even though it was only a warm up, the music was soft and mellow, other times bright and heavy, filling the room with the glorious sound of a Stradivarius violin. Arnie was in wonderment. How was this eight year old playing the instrument so eloquently, like a professional? After a few minutes the warm up was completed. The violin was put down and a music book was opened to where Mr. Mininsky, his former teacher, had been working with Israel.

The book had a dozen different pieces of music for the violin. In the three years of lessons with the teacher, Israel had worked on some of them with very few mistakes.

He was comfortable with Barcarolle, Beethoven's 5th Symphony, Blue Danube Waltz, Chopin Ballade #1, Minuet in G, Musetta's La Boheme, with his favorite being Tchaikovsky's Theme from Swan Lake. It was the first piece he'd mastered. He could remember his teacher saying, "We'll complete one piece before we go to the next. For your age, Israel, you have a unique gift, one I have never seen before! With few mistakes, you play like someone much older. But you must continue to practice, for perfection, every day if you want to continue being a very special musician!"

With this, Israel opened the page to Swan Lake. He picked up the violin and started to play. Arnie was amazed a few minutes ago during the warm up. Now, he was in shock. He thought to himself, 'this little guy is playing such beautiful music! I don't even know what he's playing but I know a great sound when I hear it!' Mother Jenny had her usual smile of approval as she did every day Israel practiced. But today was special, her son played splendidly. Maybe because of Arnie's presence or maybe it was just one of those days. In any case, it didn't matter, she was proud.

After Swan Lake, the musician lifted his arms in the air to signal he was finished. Everyone clapped hardily, even the little tots on the floor. Arnie couldn't believe what he had just heard from his new friend. When the approval died down and everyone went back to their normal activities, Arnie grabbed Israel's arm and pulled him aside saying, "Not only do you play well, you play great, like a professional! If I ever see you catching a ball or anything else that could hurt those hands, I'm going to knock your block off! I'm going to be your personal manager and bodyguard from now on. I'm going to watch you like a hawk!"

Israel felt good about Arnie's concern. They laughed and shook hands to bind the contract, which would end up lasting a lifetime.

Arnie began pushing his 'client.' "Hey Izzy, you gotta get in that Talent Contest, you'll win it hands down!"

"Arnie, first of all, we don't know if kids can enter and I'm sure it's for first class only," said Israel. "And besides, it asked for singers and dancers... I don't do either!"

"Now, you're just making excuses," answered his new business manager. "Do you mind if I ask them for you tomorrow?"

"It's okay with me," was the answer. The boys agreed to meet on the deck in the morning. They shook hands and each went their own way.

CHAPTER 6

The next morning the two boys met as usual; Israel calm and collected and Arnie excited like a kid in a candy store. "Okay my friend, let's go find out about the Talent Contest," was first thing out of Arnie's mouth. The boys headed up the stairs to the first class section. As luck would have it, the purser on duty was away from the gate talking to other people. With his back to the boys, Israel and Arnie slipped past the gate, avoiding everyone and headed for the stage where the orchestra was setting up. Israel sat in a chair as Arnie headed to the stage to speak to the leader. When he got there, Arnie extended his hand as he said, "Good morning sir, I'm Arnold Hartmanoff, can anyone enter the Talent Contest?"

"Why yes, if they pass the tryout," answered the leader. "Could that include a kid?" asked Arnie.

"Well, we've rarely had a child perform for us, but I'm sure if you pass the tryout it would be okay," answered the leader.

"Oh! It's not for me, it's for my... my... cousin,

seated over there." Arnie pointed to Israel.

"I see, a little bashful, eh?" the man questioned. "Can it be someone from economy?" asked Arnie.

"Economy? Economy? Now we've got a problem!" shouted the leader. "I'll tell you this, sir, you won't be sorry, he's very good!" shot back Arnie. "Well, let's meet this young man, send him over to me," the officer ordered.

Arnie waved to Israel, who quickly got up and headed for the stage. The orchestra leader held out his hand as he said, "Hello, young man, my name is Warrant Officer Sutton, I'm the orchestra leader and entertainment officer."

"How do you do sir, my name is Israel Turowofsky," shot back the young musician.

"Arnie here, tells me you want to be in the Talent Show," barked the officer. "Yes sir, if you think I'm good enough," replied Israel.

The officer rubbed his chin and asked, "What do you do? Sing? Dance?" "No sir, I play the violin."

"Violin! Violin! How old are you, young man?" "Eight!" replied Israel.

"Eight? How long have you been playing the violin?" "Three years, sir," replied Israel.

"You're telling me you started playing when you were five?" "Yes sir."

"Well, I'll be damned... I gotta see this! There's a little problem about being in economy because the show is for first class only, but I don't care, I'm just going to break some rules, we'll work around it somehow!" barked the officer. "Tell you what... come to tomorrow's ten am tryout, we'll see how it goes!" the officer ordered.

"Yes sir, they both replied, where do we go?"

"Report to the First Class Auditorium, across from the main dining room. And here, you'll need this pass to get into first class," offered the Officer to Israel.

"Sir, can I also have a pass for my friend Arnie?" asked Israel. Arnie lowered his face, embarrassed, knowing that the truth about their relationship was out. The officer held back a smile as he said, "Now what is he, your cousin or your best friend?"

Immediately Israel answered, "He's my best friend, (and business manager, he thought but didn't say) we're so close, he's almost my cousin!"

The officer couldn't hold back any longer, he burst out into a hearty laugh saying, "Okay, friend-cousin, here's your pass."

Arnie reached out and said, "Thank you sir."

The officer then patted each boy on the head saying, "You two remind me of my boys back home in New York, Richie and Gary, one is nine, the other twelve. I can picture them pulling the same stunt!"

Both boys shook the officer's hand as they said, "So long, see ya tomorrow!" Excitedly, the boys ran off. The rest of the day, Israel was practicing his music. But what was he going to tell his mother about the whole incident? After much thought, Israel decided to say nothing about the show to anyone. After all, he might not be selected for the show anyway, so why worry about it now?

The next day, the boys arrived at the auditorium ten minutes late. They had lost their way crossing through the First Class Dining Room. There were about fifty people seated, mostly adults, listening to the orchestra leader.

At a second glance, Israel noticed a few children accompanied by adults, probably parents. The officer was standing in front of the orchestra saying, "The Talent Show will be in five days, this coming Saturday night at 7:30 PM, here in the auditorium. It's the last social event aboard ship before we arrive in New York, Monday morning, and I'm sure it will be a packed house. Unfortunately, we can only select twelve of you to perform. With this large crowd showing up, it's possible we won't get to all of you, I hope you understand. The twelve selected will be asked to come back tomorrow at 10 AM, for one more rehearsal to polish up. As we call your name, please come up to the stage. If anyone here has not yet registered, please quickly go over to the Registration Desk and sign in."

Israel and Arnie rushed over to sign in, then returned to their seats. The tryouts began. Most were very good but a few were not. When each was finished, quietly the leader spoke to those performers. Some shook his hand and smiled, others just turned and walked away. After two hours of tryouts, Israel and two others were left, a man and a woman. The officer looked at his watch as he approached the final group saying, "I'm sorry folks, you were the last to sign in and there just isn't any more time. I've got to get these musicians to their regular duty stations." The man got up and left, saying nothing. The woman stood up saying, "It's okay, I probably wouldn't have made it, anyway," as she strolled away.

Disappointed, Israel sat with his head lowered, a tear in his eye. Arnie blurted out, "Sir, you've got to give him a chance, he was so excited about the tryout! And besides, you don't need the orchestra for him, Israel plays on his own! Please, sir, just give him a few minutes," continued Arnie.

Again, the officer looked at his watch saying, "Okay young man, give me something quick!" Israel nervously went to the stage. The officer sat in the front next to Arnie. Israel felt his body shaking. This was the first time he had ever played for a complete stranger and more importantly, one who was going to judge him. He started to play and the violin sound started to relax the young musician. As he played more, he gained more confidence and he started to hear his usual quality of music. He was doing nicely with a slight smile on his face, then he hit a few wrong notes. He started to become nervous again and hit more wrong notes. He stopped, saying nothing and lowered his head. The officer came to him, bent down and said, "Israel, I want to tell you two things. First of all, you're in the show, so relax!" Arnie let out a cheerful yell as Israel smiled ear to ear. "I want you to play for me again and this time just forget about everything else except your music. I said you're in the show, so there's nothing to worry about. Let's try it again."

Arnie gave a wink and Israel started again. The sound was completely different. Israel felt completely different. The sounds from the violin were beautiful. The officer smiled as the young musician continued. Israel's arm movements were firm and articulate, yet graceful, like a swan from *Swan Lake*. The music came to a beautiful crescendo and ended. As was his custom, when happy with his playing, Israel's arms went up, raising his bow and violin in the air, with a smile on his face. The officer slowly got up, extending his hand as he approached Israel. "Now that's more like it! I know a little something about the violin, I played it years back and I must tell you young man, you're quite good! And for working so hard, you don't have to come back tomorrow! I'll see you Saturday night, right here!"

For the first time all morning, Israel spoke. "Sir, can my family come watch me play?"

"Certainly," answered the officer. "Let me make out a pass for you. Now tell me how many are in the family?"

Israel quickly spoke up. "There's my mother, two sisters, Ida and Sadi, and my little brother Herman!"

The officer smiled and asked, "What about you cousin Arnie, here?" "Oh yea, and cousin Arnie too!" replied Israel.

"Okay, boys, here you are, passes for five for your immediate family, plus one for Arnie and three more for any other "relatives" you dig up between now and Saturday," he said with a grin. "Tell your mother to take any of the reserved seats in the front row. We save them for ship's officers, which is about twenty, but there's always plenty left, take whatever you need!" "Thank you Sir, for everything," quipped Israel, his heart beating a mile a minute.

"See you Saturday," answered the officer as he waved and hurried off.

CHAPTER 7

'Now to tell Mom and the family,' thought Israel. Israel called his mother over to a quiet corner. He explained, "Mom, I auditioned for the ship's Talent Show and made it. I'm in the show Saturday night!"

"But how could you do that, Israel... isn't it something for first class only?" she asked.

"Well, normally yes, but Arnie asked the Orchestra Leader and he made an exception. Mom, he said I was very good! And gave me special first class passes for you and all the kids. You even have reserved seats!" belted out the boy.

His mother, with a gleam in her eye leaned forward and asked, "Israel, is this what you want to do?"

"Yes... yes," answered Israel, "I really want to!"

"Okay my son, then we'll be there to watch," his mother answered. Israel ran up on deck to tell Arnie.

When Monday came, starting that afternoon and continuing twice a day for the rest of the week, Israel practiced feverishly to bring his music to the highest level he had ever reached. Arnie knew why the musician wasn't up on deck playing with the boys. Israel now played with a ray of confidence, knowing if he did his best, he would be fine. He had to be sure his nerves didn't enter into it. And the way to keep from getting nervous was to practice, practice, practice, until he knew every note was perfect.

It seemed like eternity, the days crawling from Tuesday to Saturday. Finally, Saturday arrived and Israel knew it was best not to practice that day. He wanted to be fresh for the show. He couldn't sit still, bouncing from one place to another with he, Arnie, and other boys running in and out of their quarters all day. Late in the afternoon, all the boys wished him well before each wandered off to get ready for dinner.

At mealtime, Israel hardly ate a thing, it just wouldn't go down. After some coaxing from his mother, he finally ate some toast and tea. Following dinner, everyone washed up, dressed in their Sunday best and waited until 7:30 rolled around. At 7:30 sharp, Arnie burst in, ready to go. The boys waved goodbye to friends and family who following in a few minutes, then headed for first class. When they arrived at the auditorium, it was three quarters full with people still scurrying in looking for the best seats.

The boys headed for the front row where they spotted several dozen reserved seats. They took their seats. A few minutes later, the family arrived, everyone bursting with excitement. They noticed the orchestra leader headed their way. He extended his hand to Israel's mother saying, "Mrs. Turowofsky and family, welcome! I'm Officer Sutton, the Orchestra Leader." Mother returned the greeting and offered her thanks for his help in putting all this together for her son. "My pleasure, no problem, we're excited to have him. I was just telling the orchestra, in my twenty years as a musician, I've never seen anyone as young as your son play an instrument so well. They're all looking forward to hearing him." Pointing to Israel he said, "Now, you have to go with the other contestants in the place behind the stage called the green room, that's where you wait until your name is called. Come with me, I'll show you where it is. Good luck, folks," the officer shouted to the family, as he and Israel strolled away.

CHAPTER 8

Israel entered the room where ten other people were seated. The officer said to another officer, "Herb, this is the young violin player." Israel nodded. Since his last name begins with a 'T' Israel was told to sit at the end. That's where he went, being told, "The participants will be called to the stage alphabetically." This meant Israel would go last. A few more people checked in and were told where to sit. Officer Herbert spoke, "Okay folks, as I call your name and what you do, please answer, 'Here!'

Albert Bensky - joke teller."

"Here!"

"Sylvan Bernard - Irish tenor."

"Here!"

"Mary and Margaret Catoff - singing duet."

"Here!"

"Irene Curio - operatic soprano."

"Here!"

"Leonard Duree - harmonica player."

"Here!"

"Lestri Dennano - Latin singer."

"Here!"

"Barry Frankhart - piano player."

"Here!"

"Helene Girtivitz - voice imitator."

"Here!"

"Sylvan Jackmansky - baritone."

"Here!"

"Mary Marshall - flutist."

"Here!"

"Henry Prader - tap dancer."

"Here!"

"And Israel Turowofsky - violin player."

A small voice answered, "Here!"

The group laughed, politely. Officer Herbert continued and pointed, "That left stage door will be left open and you will hear each other as you perform. When you are finished, take a bow and then take a seat in one of the chairs on stage left. After the last person performs, we will await the decision of the judges, three officers seated on the other side of the stage. There will be three winners. Third place, second place, and the grand prize winner! Each winner will receive a souvenir for their effort. Officer Sutton, our Orchestra Leader, will call your name and introduce you after a fanfare from the orchestra. As I said before, we will call you alphabetically. Is everyone ready?" Everyone gave a strong reply. Officer Herbert took a seat in the rear of the room.

The orchestra finished a cheerful medley and ended to a warm applause. The Orchestra Leader then explained to the audience details about the Talent Show and then called the first contestant.

When Albert Bensky walked out to the stage, Israel started to feel nervous. He was the only child contestant there and he hoped he wasn't in over his head. But the Orchestra Leader had said he was good! Israel squirmed in his seat as each performer took their turn. Most were very good with a few exceptions. All of the singers were wonderful and received the most applause. As the group dwindled down, it was Henry Prader's turn, the tap dancer. Israel listened to his dancing feet, each touching the floor in perfect rhythm. The young violin player quickly realized the dancer was not only good, he was terrific, and probably would be the grand prize winner. Henry received a roaring ovation. Concentrating on Henry's talent, Israel forgot about his own nervousness. Before he realized it, the Orchestra Leader was on the stage announcing the young violinist's name.

"And now, our last and youngest performer, eight year old Israel Turowofsky and his violin!" Israel stood up, with violin and bow in his hand and felt numb. He walked slowly to the stage door. He was blinded from the glare of the floodlights. At first, he could not see anything, but quickly his eyes adjusted to the lights. He then saw a packed auditorium clapping for him. He didn't know why, he hadn't even started yet. He could see Arnie and the family standing up cheering, making the most noise. Israel looked at the Orchestra Leader who gave him a nod. The violin was raised to the chin and the applause died down. Israel started to play. He had decided to put together a medley of his best music, a little something for everyone. As he played and gained confidence, he really started to feel comfortable, still a little nervous, but a good kind of nervous. One that tends to keep you sharp!

While he played, members of the orchestra were whispering to each other, while pointing to the young violinist. Israel hit a wrong note, then another, but continued and the audience never noticed. Now, he was even more confident. Previously, when making a mistake, he would stop and then start again. Not today! Today, he was playing like a professional. He felt it, felt it in his bones. He played beautifully. The young violinist then came to a strong crescendo, ending with his arms, violin and bow in the air. The crowd was standing with thunderous applause. The family and Arnie were dancing around and clapping. Israel knew he had done well. He bowed and took his seat.

CHAPTER 9

While the judges were tallying up the votes, Officer Sutton was talking to the audience about getting all their belongings together tomorrow, Sunday, to get ready for landing in New York City on Monday morning. "After twenty four days at sea, everyone has a lot of work to do before we land." The judges signaled that they were ready. Officer Sutton asked all of the performers to come to the center of the stage as he announced the winners. "Third prize goes to Irene Curio, our operatic soprano!" As she came forward, she was presented with a silver cup engraved Third Place Winner – *Noranikoff* Talent Show. Officer Sutton continued. "Second place winner... Henry Prader our dancing feet tap dancer!" His prize was a bronze model replica of the ship engraved Second Place Winner – *Noranikoff* Talent Show. "And our grand prize winner is Israel Turowofsky, our Russian fiddler!"

The auditorium erupted into a standing ovation. Israel was stunned! He couldn't speak, felt even a little faint. Officer Sutton handed him a twelve inch gold replica of the Statue of Liberty, engraved Grand Prize Winner – *Noranikoff* Talent Show – Welcome to America! Israel was too dazed to talk. He just smiled and shook the officer's hand. Officer Sutton bent over to the young musician saying, "I expect to read about you in the papers! Please remember me when you become famous!"

"Thank you sir, thanks for everything, believe me, I'll always remember you!" replied Israel.

All of the performers gathered around the young musician and wished him well. He thanked each, then headed to his family and Arnie. They all smothered him with kisses and hugs and wouldn't stop clapping. Arnie watched from the side, saying nothing. After a few moments, Israel ran to him and gave him a tremendous hug. They both danced around yelling, "What a night, what a night!" Arnie added, "My little man, you're just getting started, they ain't seen nothing yet!"

CHAPTER 10

Sunday was a work day, collecting all the things left around the ship after twenty four days at sea. Passengers gathered up books, magazines, games, puzzles, and everything else friends had borrowed. After packing and final goodbyes to friends and neighbors, everyone went to bed early, awaiting the ship's 6 AM arrival in America. Before going to bed, Arnie and Israel embraced in a final farewell. Arnie swore he'd find his new but very close friend if they both were in the same city. Both boys had watery eyes.

Israel awoke to the loud horn of the ship *Noranikoff's* stack. The ship was calling to the tugboats that she had arrived. Everyone who could find an open porthole, watched the giant ship pass the Statue of Liberty. The tugboats hugged her firmly as they gently guided *Noranikoff* to the mooring. They had arrived in America!

After several hours of unloading cargo, the horn blew signaling the start of passenger debarking. The ship's passengers were divided into sections and were told where and when to leave the ship. The first class passengers started leaving the ship from the upper gangplank, an orderly line of handsomely dressed people escorted by their personal ship stewards carrying their luggage. After a rather long wait, the ship's horn blasted twice, signaling the start of economy debarking. Everyone carried their own luggage with many parents also carrying their babies. It was a very gradual, slow moving line just getting to the gangplank. And again, a slow moving line down the gangplank until you touched the United States of America!

Once on solid ground, everyone smiled with a sigh of relief, but more lines were just beginning. There was the enormous line into the Immigration Building, where Mother Jenny carried little Herman in one arm, while holding both daughters' hands in the other. The girls carried all the luggage except Israel's.

Israel carried his suitcase in one hand and his violin case in the other. He was having a hard time keeping up with his sisters but so far he could see them okay. After an hour of tugging and pushing, they finally arrived at the Immigration Desk designated for the letter 'T.' Jenny gave a sigh of relief. The officer said, "Welcome to the United States!" Jenny could have kissed him. Putting Herman down, Jenny told the girls to sit on their luggage while she spoke to the immigration officer. She turned to tell Israel the same thing, he wasn't there! Frantically, she called "Israel! Israel!" The boy did not answer. She turned to the officer screaming, "I've lost my son, I've lost my son!"

The officer tried to calm her and then called over a lady attendant to try and help.

The attendant pulled Jenny and the children aside, Jenny was crying frantically. She called out again, "Israel! Israel! Where are you?" No child answered. The lady sat Jenny down and explained, "Often we lose children, this is such a big place, but we always find them." Jenny continued to sob as her children hung on with frightened concern. The attendant pulled out her pad and pen, asking the mother some questions. "Please give me the child's name, age, size, and general description. I'll relay it to all the stations. This is Station 1, we have twelve more all the way down the line. I know one of our stations will pick him up. Now, I know it's hard, but try to relax."

Jenny took some deep breaths and tried to think clearly. She thought the lady had to be right, someone would find him and take him to one of the stations. The thought calmed her down, somewhat. The attendant continued, "Why don't we finish going through Immigration. I'll take you to the front of the line and when we're through, we'll start looking for your little boy."

Before Jenny knew it, she and the children had cleared through Immigration, with only one small change. Their last name was now Turow instead of Turowofsky.

CHAPTER 11

Israel kept walking. He thought he was following his sisters, with people pushing and shoving in between. But when he got a clear glimpse of the girls, it wasn't them, just a family that looked similar. Israel started to walk faster. Almost running. He yelled, "Mommy! Mommy!" But no one answered. He realized he was lost. He stopped and started to cry. Someone passing called to an officer who was standing nearby. It was obvious the child was lost. The officer bent down to Israel saying reassuringly, "Don't cry little guy, we'll find your folks. I know you feel frightened and lost now, but I'll have you with your family real soon. Just tell me your name and age." Israel answered the man. The officer replied, "Okay Israel, let's go to the station and wait for your parents. I'll wire all of the other stations and before you know it, your folks will be popping in the door. They could be there waiting for us." That made the little boy smile a little. He picked up his suitcase and violin while walking off with the officer.

Once in the Station House, Israel was greeted warmly, seated and given a piece of candy. The officer then went to the teletype machine and sent out the boy's description to all the other stations. From past experience, he knew he would hear something soon. He then came back to the frightened lad, bending down, pointing and asking, "Is that some kind of an instrument in there?"

"Yes, sir, it's my violin, replied Israel.

"Is it a real violin or just a toy?" the man asked.

"It's a Grenadier Stradivarius, one of the finest violins made," answered the boy as he opened the case.

The officer was surprised to see such a handsome instrument in the hands of such a young boy. "Do you play it?" the man asked.

"Yes sir," was the reply, in a confident manner.

The man continued, "If you're eight now, when did you start playing?" With the answer of a veteran musician, Israel replied, "When I was five!" The officer was now really amazed and wanted very much to hear the little guy play. Or was this whole thing some sort of a joke? He wondered how to ask. He knew the lad was still somewhat distraught and scared.

He said softly, "You know Israel, many times we have a lost child in here and if we can get them to sing very loud, often their parents will hear them and come to the station to get them. It's just a thought but if we could get you to play the violin, it's possible someone in your family would hear you!" The boy did not feel like playing but he looked quizzically at the man and thought it might work, maybe Mommy will hear me. Slowly, the boy took the instrument out of the case and placed it under his chin. The man could see the boy knew what he was doing. The music started to flow. It was very pretty but had a sadness attached to it. Everyone in the station stopped what they were doing and turned to listen to the music from this young child.

Some even moved their seats closer. The officer, now amazed, thought, it's obvious the youngster knows what he's doing, the music sounds so professional. Israel played as loud as he could. After about ten minutes, the playing stopped. Sadly, the youngster looked up at the officer saying, "I hope my Mother heard me!"

"I did darling, I heard you all the way down the concourse," answered a familiar voice standing at the door. There, at the entrance way was Jenny, the children, and a police officer. Israel burst into tears screaming, "Mommy, Mommy!"

"My God, Israel, I was so worried, my little angel," she screamed as she ran towards him. All of the kids rushed to Israel, hugging among tears and laughter. After everyone settled down, gathered their composure and started to feel close to normal, Jenny thanked the officers many times. She then asked, "Where can we get a carriage or something to take us to the train station?"

One of the officers answered, "It's too hectic out there now ma'am, you'll wait forever. You've been through enough, we'll take you to the station." Very thankful, Jenny asked, "Are you sure you can do that, I mean, we don't want to take up any more of your time."

"No problem, ma'am, I go that way on my way home and I'm off in a few minutes," said the officer.

"How can I ever thank you people for being so helpful and kind?" offered Jenny.

"No problem, ma'am, that's what we're here for, but another tune from this young man would sure be nice," answered the officer.

Without hesitation, Israel ran to his violin and

started to play. This time it was happy music, with warmth, beauty, and grace. When Israel was finished, his arms went up in the air, in his usual custom, and he received his second standing ovation of the week!

CHAPTER 12

Jenny and the children were escorted safe and sound to New York's Pennsylvania Station after an exciting and informative ride by one of New York's finest. After more thankyou's and goodbye's, the family rushed to the main ticket office to purchase fares to Baltimore. They also had to wire Izik and Morris that they had arrived in New York and were on their way. Izik knew the approximate time of the ship's arrival in New York, but all of the other happenings certainly had caused a delay. Izik had been checking all day with the Baltimore station's telegraph office, hoping to hear something about the family's arrival. Shortly, he would get his answer.

The excitement of the pending train ride kept the children scurrying in and out of their seats with restless chatter up and down the aisle. But soon after departure, fatigue set in and everyone was dozing, while leaning on each other. All except Israel, he couldn't sleep. His head rested on the large glass window, as he watched the towns, villages, and green meadows rush by. He was in a near sleep reverie, thinking about all the events over the last forty eight hours. It had only been two days since he last saw Arnie, but it seemed like eternity. He wondered if he would ever see him again. He thought back about the talent contest aboard the ship and the wonderful feeling he got when the audience stood to applaud him. He also was thinking how helpful and considerate the Orchestra Leader had been when he took the extra time to work with him. Israel reflected back to the time, several years ago, when his father and brother Morris started speaking English around the house. The father had learned from a coworker at the factory and his brother was taught in school. It was decided at the time that the family would try to speak only English, hoping one day they would be going to America. The young musician now knew, without knowing the English language, he probably never would have gotten into the talent show. Everyone around the show spoke English.

Slowly Israel's eyes began to close and he fell into a deep sleep. He was back on the stage playing with the orchestra accompanying him. He was playing beautifully but the Leader kept yelling, "Bali, Bali!" Why was he yelling while Israel was playing? Suddenly the yelling became louder and louder. Startled, Israel opened his eyes and jumped up. He saw the back of a large man passing down the aisle yelling,

"Baltimore, Baltimore, next stop Baltimore!"

He now understood who was doing the yelling in his dream. Quickly, Jenny woke all the children and got them ready for their arrival in Baltimore.

Everyone was excited and looking forward to seeing their father and big brother. It had been nearly a month since they all said their goodbyes to each other. The train started to slow down as it bellowed a loud whistle. Everyone was grabbing their belongings, getting ready to move off the train. Israel grabbed his violin and suitcase tightly. He was ready to start his new life.

The conductor helped Jenny and the children off the train. The mother started to look around but a familiar voice filled the air. "Jenny, Jenny Dear!" She turned and saw Izik and Morris running towards them. She hadn't spoken to or seen her husband and oldest son for over a month and could not hold back the tears.

"Daddy, Morris," the children screamed as they ran towards the men. It was a joyous reunion having the whole family together again.

After gathering their luggage and belongings, Izik led the way out of the station. He had borrowed a friend's automobile for the trip to the new home on Collington Ave in East Baltimore. The house belonged to Izik's brother Sam, a widower, who was looking forward to his new family. He was lonely since the passing of his wife last year. While the chatter in the car flowed freely back and forth between the family, Israel sat quietly, deep in thought.

As he viewed the homes, stores, and people of downtown Baltimore, he was troubled. It didn't matter where he slept or the size of the room. It didn't matter about making new friends or going to the new school. Only one thing mattered to Israel at the moment.

As they passed Eastern Ave and Patterson Park, they soon came to Collington and pulled up to a row house in the middle of the block. Every house on the street had gleaming white marble steps in front. The block looked like one very large house with dozens of doorways and steps leading into it. Uncle Sam greeted the family with open arms.

After a few minutes to sit and catch their breath, he led them to the kitchen. Dinner was ready. The family hadn't had a real meal in two days. The table looked like a banquet. Barley soup so thick you could eat it with a fork, roast stuffed chicken, assorted breads, mashed potatoes, peas, carrots, and three assorted fruit pies. God bless Uncle Sam! The family was starved and almost ate themselves sick. At the end, the adults had coffee and the children had milk with their dessert.

When their bellies were full, Uncle Sam said to Israel, "Your mother wrote to me several times, telling me how well you're doing with the violin. I hope you'll play for me sometime." Israel looked up, thinking it was a delicious meal, I really enjoyed it, but how do I tell Uncle Sam what's worrying me?

CHAPTER 13

After dinner the family gathered in the living room to separate their belongings. After much conversation, Uncle Sam showed everyone to their rooms. Sam had the master bedroom, in the rear on the third floor, facing the backyard and garden. Jenny and Izik had the other third floor bedroom, facing the front. Both bedrooms shared a large bathroom in the middle of the hall. On the second floor, Ida and Sadi shared the rear bedroom, while little Herman and Israel had the front room. Again, both second floor bedrooms shared a hall bath.

Because Morris was the eldest, he was rewarded the basement quarters which consisted of a double bed, sofa, desk, chair, and kitchen set. He also had his own entrance, which offered some privacy. The house had plenty of room for everyone. The extra bedrooms belonged to Sam's children who lived there before they were married. Before bedtime, Uncle Sam stopped by everyone's room to be sure everyone was comfortable and had any needs. He came to Herman and Israel's room last. "Is everything okay?" he questioned.

Herman was already under the covers saying, "I'm in dreamland." Israel nodded approvingly but had concern on his face. He blurted out, "Uncle Sam, back home in Russia, I had a little place in the corner of the living room to practice my violin. It wasn't always the most convenient but we worked it out. Can you think of a place I can practice here, without getting in the way?"

Uncle Sam rubbed his chin, scratched his head, and finally said regrettably, "I'm not sure what we can do Israel." Jenny and Izik were peeking in the door, smiling to themselves. There was a smirk on Uncle Sam's face as he offered, "Let's have a look around!" He led Israel out of the room, as if he wasn't sure where to go. "Let's start downstairs first, maybe we can find an empty closet!" blurted Sam.

The young boy thought to himself, closet? What can I do in a closet? Sam led the way downstairs to the kitchen. He continued into the back pantry and opened a door. Uncle Sam said to Israel, "Take a look in there!" Israel slowly stepped into the small room. His eyes widened to a glorious setting. A beautiful floor lamp lit up the room which faced the rear garden.

There was a music stand with a chair, plus a desk and another chair. Musical themed pictures were scattered around the walls. While the young musician stood in amazement. Uncle Sam asked, "Think this will work out, Israel?" Without saying a word, Israel ran into Sam's arms. Uncle Sam got the biggest hug and kiss he had gotten in a long time.

"You knew what was bothering me all the time, didn't you Uncle Sam?" bellowed Israel.

"I think so," replied the uncle. He added, "This was Aunt Sara's old sewing room. I thought it would be well used if we converted it to a music room. I know she's looking down and smiling at you right now!

Oh, by the way, the card on the desk is the name and phone number of my neighbor, Ben Hershey. He's a retired music teacher from the Peabody Institute here in Baltimore. That's one of the finest music schools in the area. Only the best talent goes there. He now teaches violin and piano part time. He's heard all about you and he's ready to help whenever you call.

He's a friend of mine, owes me some favors, so there's no cost to you. Call him, you'll like him!" exclaimed Sam. Uncle Sam got his second biggest hug and kiss for the day. Through all of this, Jenny and Izik were peeking through the small door, smiling to themselves. They had known all along about Sam's surprise for Israel. They hoped and prayed the surprise would be a factor in the young boy's future career. They knew Israel's future was music.

CHAPTER 14

It took the whole next day for everyone to catch up on their sleep. They were totally exhausted. Each one got up only to get something to eat and then back to bed. But finally, the cobwebs wore away and the family started somewhat of a normal routine. Jenny and Izik went shopping for groceries and other necessities. The children played around the house or in the garden. Uncle Sam was the babysitter. Israel was in the music room, practicing the violin. He had called Ben Hershey. Ben was due there in an hour.

The doorbell chimed and Sam greeted Ben warmly. They came back to the kitchen. As they opened the door to the music room, Israel was concentrating on his playing. He did not see the two men as they slipped into the room quietly. Ben studied the small boy who was playing beautifully. After several minutes, Israel came to a pause and looked up in surprise. "Please don't stop playing, I'm enjoying listening to you. I'm Ben Hershey," said the teacher.

Israel shook his hand, responding, "Very nice to meet you sir." Israel continued to play. Uncle Sam had disappeared moments earlier. Ben looked over the boy's stance, his arm movements, his body position and the quick movement of fingers of the small hands. In all the years teaching at Peabody, he could not remember someone so young, playing so well. But the boy's stance needed improvement. The body position to the instrument and the width of the feet were incorrect. Yet it was amazing how well the boy played even with the deficiencies. Ben had a feeling he had a good one here. He guessed the boy might become something special. When Israel finished playing, he raised his fiddle and bow in the air and smiled at the teacher.

Ben asked, "How long have you been playing the violin, Israel?" "Since I was five," the boy answered.

"How old are you now?" the teacher asked. "I'm eight and a half," answered the boy.

"I think you play quite well, considering the short time you have been playing. Tell me, do you know much about the violin, I mean where it came from and how it works?" Ben asked.

The answer was, "I, I, think so, I mean..."

The teacher interrupted, saying, "Let me tell you this, there's a wonderful history to the violin, much I'm sure you don't know about. What makes the beautiful sound? It might be a little complicated for you now at your young age, but in a minute, I'll try to explain it to you." Ben did not want to overwhelm the boy and possibly loose his interest. He thought it best to let the student express himself. "Tell me Israel, do you have any idea what happens when the bow touches the strings?"

"I think so, sir" answered the boy.

Ben smiled at the boy's manner. He already liked the student and wanted to encourage him. "Don't worry if you can't explain it all, just tell me what you think," said the teacher.

CHAPTER 15

"Well sir, when the bow touches the strings, the bridge acts as the transmitter that carries the string's vibrations to the belly of the violin, where the soundboard can be found. The soundboard is supported by a bass bar, a narrow wooden bar that runs lengthwise into the belly. A soundpost, a cylinder usually made from pine, sits inside the instrument, under the treble foot of the bridge and between the belly and the back, and carries the sound further into the instrument's back. This gives the violin its characteristic sound and tone. When the violin's strings are plucked or drawn with a bow, the vibrations travel down this path and reverberate within the instrument, producing the sound you hear—a sound hauntingly similar to the human voice. The strength of the attack creates a crescendo or decrescendo of sound," replied the boy.

For five seconds Ben stared at the boy in amazement, before choking out the words, "Very good Israel. Tell me son, do you know where the violin came from, I mean, where it got its start?"

"I think so, sir," was the answer. "The violin

belongs to the family of chordophones, a classification within the Sachs-Hornbostel system, which was devised to categorize instruments that produce sound through the vibration of strings. Chordophones are further divided into four subtypes: lutes, zithers, lyres, and harps. The violin is a member of the sub-category lutes, because of its narrow neck, which protrudes from the resonating body, as well as its strings, which run along the neck to tuning pegs.

Because stringed instruments are made from wood, an easily perishable material, their history before written language is largely unknown. Our knowledge of early violins is limited to the ancient cultures of East and South Asia, Mesopotamia, and the Mediterranean."

"Historians depend solely on iconographic sources as there are no surviving specimens. The closest relative of the modem violin was born in Italy, and its creators were Gasparo da Salo, Andrea Amati, and Giovanni Paolo Maggini. This trio set proportions used in modem instruments by the end of the 16th century. Earlier instruments are recognizable by their deeply arched bellies and backs: this group's newer violins were shallower, producing a larger, louder tone. Makers such as Antonio Stradivari, perfected these early designs into the instrument we know today. By the way, my violin, which was my grandfather's, is a

Stradivarius, Mr. Hershey," Israel replied.

Again, the teacher stared at the student. After a moment of silence, he asked, "Where did you learn about the violin, young man?"

The boy replied, "From Mr. Mininsky, my teacher in Russia."

"He must have been a very good teacher Israel, he taught you well!" answered Ben.

"Yes sir, we practiced every day after school for several hours and after dinner, I practiced again by myself. I love playing the violin," was Israel's reply.

Ben sat back, rubbed his chin as he murmured to himself, "I'm wrong, this young man isn't going to be special... he's very special right now!"

CHAPTER 16

It was Thursday afternoon, on a beautiful mid-June day. The music teacher and the student had been working very hard all week trying to familiarize themselves with each other. They had accomplished a lot and still the young student was eager for more. Ben Hershey looked out back at the sunny rose garden, remembering how lovely this time of year was. With school over for the summer, most of the local children would be playing in the park, just a few blocks away. Israel had just finished playing a piece for the teacher. When the boy looked up, his eyes seemed tired. Ben asked, "Have you met any new friends? Have you been to the park?"

"Not yet," answered the boy. "I've been too busy with my music and working around the house."

"I want you to do me a favor," replied Ben. "I want you to stay away from the violin Friday, Saturday, and Sunday. Have your parents take you to the park. You'll meet new friends, you'll enjoy it. It's important that you give yourself a rest from the music for a few days. That way, when you start again Monday, you'll be rested, it'll be fresh to you, and you'll enjoy it more.

Will you do that for me, Israel?"

The young boy answered, "I'll try, sir. I've never been away from the violin that long."

"Let's give it a try and see what happens," replied Ben.

It was agreed that Israel was to find other things to do over the weekend. At dinner that evening, Jenny promised to take Israel to Patterson Park Friday morning to look around. The boy could have gone himself, since the park was only a few blocks away but his mother felt better taking him the first time.

Friday morning, after breakfast, Israel sat out on the front steps eagerly waiting for his mother to come out. As he sat there, a boy seemingly his age strolled by. In a friendly manner, the stranger said, "Hi, I'm Eugene Silverman. I've never seen you around before, you just moved here?"

"Yes, we just moved in a few days ago. I'm Israel Turow. You can call me Izzy."

"You can call me Gene. Where did you move from?" he asked as they shook hands.

"Russia," Israel replied.

"Russia? That's far away, isn't it?" Gene questioned.

"All I know is, after leaving Russia, we were on the ship for almost two months... that's what it seemed like!" Israel answered.

"Well, welcome to America, Izzy, I'm heading to the park. Want to go with me?" asked Gene.

"Yes, wait a minute while I tell my mother," was the reply. Israel scurried inside for a moment and returned quickly.

Jenny came to the door to peek out. She saw the two boys walking away talking and laughing as they headed off to play. She felt good, her son had made his first American friend.

CHAPTER 17

As the boys came to the end of the block, ready to cross, coming up the adjacent street were friends of Gene, the three Benesh sisters, Julia, Rachel, and Beatrice. Julia was the oldest, Gene's age. She waved when she saw him. As they got closer, Gene said, "Hi girls, this is Israel Turow. He just moved here from Russia."

Israel interrupted, saying, "My friends call me Izzy... nice to meet you." The first thing Israel noticed on the girl his age, was her beautiful dark hair with long curls. Her sweet smile and pleasant face caught his eye.

She offered her hand and said, "I'm Julia. These are my sisters, Rachel and Beatrice."

Rachel quickly replied, "Our friends call us Rhey and Bibi." "Hello again," answered Israel. "Do you live nearby?" "Down Collington, near the drugstore," Julia answered.

"I'm on Collington too, I'm sure we'll be seeing each other around," answered Israel.

"I'm sure we will," replied the girl. They waved

goodbye, as the girls continued their stroll around the block. The boys headed for the park. As the boys approached Eastern Avenue, they came to the edge of Patterson Park and stood on the overlook viewing down at the vast valley of children playing. Israel was amazed at the size of the area, the amount of people and the variety of games and activities that were going on. There was baseball, soccer, kickball, volleyball, kite flying, and some kids just milling around. Some boys were throwing around an oblong ball that Israel did not recognize. Gene pointed, saying, "Let's go down to the touch football game! I'll introduce you to the guys!" Izzy and Gene trotted down to the group.

Gene made introductions. Then someone shouted from the back of the group, "Holy shit! Izzy is that you?" Coming forward with his hand extended was Arnie Hartmanoff, his old shipmate.

Izzy bellowed out, "Arnie, Arnie, I don't believe it!" They both hugged and patted each other as they danced around screaming in their delight.

Gene yelled, "When are you buying furniture?"

Arnie shouted, "Shut up! Hey guys, meet my shipmate and buddy, Izzy Turowofsky!"

Israel shouted. "It's now Turow! They changed it at Ellis Island!" "They changed mine to Hartman!" was

Arnie's retort.

CHAPTER 18

Because they were older and bigger, Arnie and Sol generally were the ones to pick sides. Sol blurted out "Luki!" Arnie followed, "Gene!" The two leaders kept choosing until they were down to the last two, Lenny Benesh and Israel.

Sol said, "Little Lenny!" who generally was always last, mainly because he was the smallest and youngest. And, the only reason he was chosen at all was because he had three pretty sisters, Julie, Rhey, and Bibi Benesh.

Sometimes, groups of girls would stroll by and often the Benesh girls were part of the group. Then Arnie spoke up, "Okay, I'll take Izzy Turowo..." "Turow!" Israel instantly corrected him!"

"Wait a minute, you can't play Izzy... you can't take a chance with those hands!"

The boys were puzzled. "What are you talking about Arnie?"

Arnie tried to explain. "Izzy is a violin player, I mean some kind of player! I mean the best... he can't take a chance of hurting those fingers and hands!"

Israel was confused. How could I hurt my hands? Arnie tried to explain the game, touch football included running, catching, blocking, etc., then added, "Why don't you sit out and watch for a few minutes... we'll get you in, in a little while!"

"Okay," Izzy replied, "whatever you think!"

The game started and Israel got excited while watching the action. He didn't understand all the rules but he liked what he saw. It looked great to him! A few minutes later, a group of girls strolled by. At times they would cheer the boys on and mingle with them during some of the brakes. At one point, Gene limped out.

"Go in for me Izzy, I turned my ankle!"

"Okay" Izzy ran out. When he got into the huddle, Arnie said, "Izzy, just do what I tell you each play, don't be hitting anybody!"

Israel followed instructions but mostly kept away from any contact. As the game went on, Israel liked it!

Late in the game with the score tied, on a kick-off from Sol's team, the ball made a funny bounce and landed in Israel's hands. Arnie hollered, "Follow me!" The boys skirted around to the right, Arnie blocking the way. Soon, Izzy found he could move around Arnie just by running faster. Izzy ran as fast as he could, passing the opponents one by one and reaching the goal line untouched. All the boys ran over, "Izzy, Izzy, where did you get those wheels?" They all patted him on the back. "Great run, we won, we won, you broke the tie! Hell of a run, Turow!" The game was over.

As the boys came to the sidelines, a familiar looking girl with long curls came closer, gave her little brother Lenny a hug, then turned and said to Izzy. "Great run, remember we met earlier?"

"Thank you, yes I remember, I definitely remember!" Izzy answered bashfully as he was still a little winded from the run, and explained, "This is my first time playing this game, I've got a lot to learn but I love it!"

The pretty girl answered, "I'm sure it won't be the last! And just in case you forgot, my name is Julia Benesh!"

CHAPTER 19

Israel looked at his watch. "Oh, my gosh, it's two-thirty, gotta run." Arnie yelled, "Yeah, you better get out of here, you're going to be late!" As Israel skirted off, Julia looked at Arnie quizzically. "What's that all about?"

Arnie tried to explain, " Izzy doesn't like to talk about it, he's a violin player and has lessons somewhere around two... and I mean to tell you, he's some kind of player! Maybe one day you'll be able to hear him."

"Hope so," she answered.

When Izzy reached the white steps of his house, his teacher was waiting and seemed angry. His teacher bellowed, "Do you know what time it is?" "Yes sir," answered Izzy, "just a few minutes after two!"

"Not a few minutes... it's two thirty, that's a half hour late," yelped the teacher.

Israel was stunned, he hadn't realized his teacher was going to be so strict about time.

"Listen to me, young man, I don't care that you're a

talented young man, no student keeps me waiting. Do you understand? One more time being late, I'm finished, do you understand? DO YOU UNDERSTAND?" Sheepishly, Izzy answered, "I'm sorry sir, it won't happen again, I promise!" It looked like Israel was going to cry.

The teacher kept his stern face for a few seconds then smiled, and said to the boy, "Let's go practice."

They entered the music room. The teacher said, "Go to your violin, take it from the case and show me how you get ready to play." Israel uncased the instrument and placed it under his chin, in his normal manner. The teacher said, "Play anything... I want to talk about your stance. For now, just play the C major scale."

The boy obliged, playing the scale perfectly.

"Okay, now put your arms down and move each foot approximately three inches wider apart and turn your body just a fraction to the right. Now place the violin under your chin, as normal. Fine, now play me the C major scale again."

The boy did so. When finished, he said to his teacher, "You know Mr. Hershey, it feels better, I like it!"

Mr. Hershey answered, "That's because when you place the instrument under your chin, which is slightly left, you even the weight of your body, making it more comfortable to play. Remembering this stance all the time, in the long run should be helpful to you. Okay, put the instrument back in the case, then take it out and show me your stance."

The boy did so perfectly.

Mr. Hershey then said, "Before getting to the music, tell me something about the violin."

The boy quickly answered, "When the bow hits the…"

"Oh my God, here we go again!" the teacher interrupted. "Alright, alright, play me all the scales, starting at C Major and ending at B Minor."

And Israel obliged running the scales.

So, the summer rolled on, playing in the park, weather perfect, sunny in the low eighties, then taking violin lessons. Not a bad life. Before long it would be time to start the new school year.

Going back several weeks, after three days of settling in the new home, one of the first orders of business was registering all the children for their new schools. After making several inquiries, Jenny was told the closest elementary school was just a block away down Collington Ave. That would take care of Israel and Herman. Morris and the girls would have to register at the junior high three blocks away. Jenny made the appointments with the principals of both schools. She was told to bring with her all the documentation she had from their Russian schools.

Dressed in their best, Jenny and the boys visited Mrs. Everest, Principal of the elementary school. Herman's and the girls' records were fine, all in proper order. The principal knew exactly where to place the children. Mail would be sent to the parents two weeks prior to school opening, with which room number to report to. For some reason, the Russian school records for Israel were not complete. He had to be tested, both written and orally. After about an hour, the tests were completed and the principal thanked Jenny and the children for their patience. Again, she repeated, "Mail will advise which room to report to." Jenny thought to herself, done, the elementary school kids were registered!

CHAPTER 20

As expected, about two weeks before Labor Day, the school letters arrived. Herman was to report to room 100 and Israel to room 210 at the elementary school. Being older, Morris and the girls were going to go to a different school.

And that's the way it started that glorious Friday just after Labor Day. Israel and Herman walked to school, with Israel making sure Herman went to the right room. It was agreed that Jenny would pick up Herman after school for his doctor's appointment. As Israel took the steps to the second floor, he heard the chatter down the hall coming from room 210. There they were, most of the boys and girls he'd hung out with from the neighborhood park, each greeting one another. Most of his closest friends since he arrived from Russia (except for Arnie who was in a higher grade) were all there in one place. Israel knew it was going to be a great school term.

After a while, a teacher came in and settled everyone down. "Alright children, take a seat and quiet down, please. My name is Mrs. Langenfelter," she said firmly. The teacher continued, "As I call your name, come up to the front of the room, making a straight line at the door. Robert Anderson, Benjamin Apner, Evelyn Aster," the teacher continued going alphabetically by the last name. "Sol Gerber... Henry Suster. Louis Swatts... William Taylor, Barbara Tedsky, Arnold Tobbins, Joyce Trucker, Henry Vicker."

Israel was waiting as the teacher passed the T's, his name was not called. He jumped up from his seat and rushed to the teacher's desk. "Mrs. Lang, you forgot my name!"

"What is your name, young man?" she asked. "Israel Turow," he answered.

She referred to a list, then looked up, saying, "It's okay, just go back to your seat for now."

Israel was stunned and confused. Something was wrong. He returned to his seat and slowly sat down. As his friends' names were called and each moved towards the front, one by one they looked back at Israel. When the teacher finished calling the names, she instructed, "Now move on down the hall to room 220. Mrs. Schields is your new teacher. You're now the new A class!" The children slowly moved out. Again, most gave one more look back at Israel, as if to say, so long friend.

The near empty room, except for one student seated

nearby, was quiet. Mrs. Langenfelter sat at her desk, reading a list, she said nothing. Soon, a group of kids came rushing in, laughing and talking as they filled the room. Israel kept his head down, feeling sad and sick, his heart ready to burst. He now knew what was happening—he was being held back in the B class. He tried as hard as he could to hold back the tears. On a quick glance he knew some of the new faces, kids from the neighborhood and park whom he didn't play with because they were younger. Israel had a terrible feeling of embarrassment and shame..

Soon the teacher put her reading down and announced, "I am Mrs. Langenfelter, welcome to my new B class!" The children returned the greeting and clapped. The teacher continued, "Because it is Friday and such a pretty day, I'm going to let you out early. Your assignment over the weekend is to bring in on Monday a newspaper article about current events. Okay, you're all dismissed!"

As the room emptied, Israel got up slowly, still not wanting to meet anyone's eyes. Once he got up, he glanced around. From the back of the room he saw someone waving. It was Julia Benesh!

Julia and Israel walked home together. Julia kept the conversation going with anything she could think of. She wanted to help him anyway she could. But Israel kept his head down and said nothing. When Chase

Street emptied into the middle of Collington Ave, each would go in different directions, he north and she south. Just as they split, Julia turned and said, "You know, Arnie Hartman thinks you're quite a musician, I mean not good but great! Generally, he doesn't exaggerate much about things... and even though I've never heard you play, I've got to think you're pretty dam good. I can't wait to hear you. One day, when you're up on that stage performing, with many of your friends in the audience... they'll be saying to themselves, 'My God, I wish I could play like that... I'd give anything to be Israel Turow!' And guess what, who'll be ahead then?"

Israel lifted his head and smiled. "Darned, thanks Julie, I swear you made me feel better, I mean it, I really feel better!" Without thinking, he reached for her hand and kissed it. Israel surprised himself with the gesture, then reached over and kissed her on the check. Then said as he walked away, "Have a great weekend, see ya Monday!"

CHAPTER 21

At 1216 East Baltimore Street, Baltimore, Maryland, the Jewish Educational Alliance (JEA) opening in 1913, became a refuge for local adults and children participating in free activities that included art, dance, and music programs plus athletic, literary, and social clubs. It also housed classrooms and voluntary doctors' offices. The JEA served thousands of Jewish residents in East Baltimore. Every day and every evening something was going on at the JEA. This was true especially in the colder months when outdoor activities were curtailed in the park. Continuous basketball games in the gym between the various clubs and meetings in the classrooms kept the building humming.

Approximately four nights a week you would find Israel Turow and his closest musical friends practicing or playing their various musical instruments in room 100, which was nicknamed the music room. Since Israel seemed to have the most experience, he was considered the leader of the room.

As time went on, this is where Israel started leading

his first orchestra. The music group would sometimes put on special music-night concerts (when the gym was available) or other times perform in outreach programs to various hospitals and charities in the area. Little by little, the JEA - Israel Turow orchestra became very popular around the East Baltimore Community.

After refereeing two club basketball games in the gym, Ron Roberts showered, changed clothes, and was ready to leave the building. When looking out the front door, the rain was pouring down. He decided to hang around a while until the weather looked better. He'd had enough basketball for the night, so he decided to walk the halls to see what was going on. After passing rooms of dancing and meetings, he came to room 100.

The music was beautiful, so he decided to drop in. Leading a group of eight young musicians was a boy playing the violin, soloing while the others filled in the background. He couldn't believe what he was hearing coming from this young man. Ron wasn't a music connoisseur but had a little music background from his older brother Sidney who taught music at the nearby Peabody Institute. Ron knew a special talent when he heard it. When he got home, he called Sidney and told him about the young musician. He didn't have a name to give him but told Sidney where to go and look for the leader playing the violin. Ron continued, "You'll know him when you hear him!" Sidney wrote the information in his little book and thanked his brother for the tip. The teacher was always on the lookout for special talent.

The Magothy River is twenty seven miles from East Baltimore. Going East on Rt 40 then south on Rt 1, you'll get there in approximately thirty minutes by car. That's what older brother Morris and three friends (Mike, Todd, and Stuart) did on that beautiful Indian summer day. With weather in the upper eighties, it was just too nice to go to school, so they took off, parents not notified. Mike had borrowed his dad's car without permission, filled it with gas, packed lunches, and off they went. Arriving at the shore, they spread out some blankets and ate lunch. After a short snooze, Mike stood up, rubbed his eyes and shouted, "Come on guys, let's swim to the wooden float!" The float was a twenty foot square resting place in deep water which was approximately two hundred yards away. They all got up, ran for the water which seemed endlessly shallow until finally getting deeper. Then, they each dove deep. Mike, Stuart, Todd, and lastly Morris.

When the three boys reached the float, they hopped on, each wiping their faces and catching their breath. Then, the boys screamed almost in unison, "Where's Morris?" They quickly checked the other three sides of the float, but no one was there. "Oh my God, Morris didn't make it," yelled Mike. "Todd, go back and call for help, we'll check the water. God, please help us, please God, please God!" He screamed as he dove into the water.

Two hundred yards in deep water is a large span to cover. The boys found nothing. Shortly the police squad car and watercraft boat arrived. Crying, the boys tried to explain everything to the officers. They knew Morris didn't leave because his wallet and keys were still on the blanket. After getting names and information, the police told the boys to go home, stay there, and be available for more information. The police boat was going to make a few runs before notifying the parents. The family was devastated waiting for a miracle. The next morning the police scuba divers found a body. It was blue all over, it was Morris Turow.

It was determined after examination. Morris's body showed no marks of abrasion, and that the probable cause of death was drowning. It was assumed that the swimmer probably got a stomach cramp while swimming. The three friends agreed that they never heard Morris call for help.

After the funeral, evening services were held in the home for the week (except for the sabbath) and the father, Israel and Herman, went to the synagogue early each morning for thirty days. Because of being in mourning, none of the children attended school or any activities at the JEA for the week.

Sidney Roberts, the Peabody teacher, not knowing the family tragedy, decided to visit the JEA on an evening that Israel was absent. Finding room 100, he slipped in and took a seat. In the front of the room were five young men playing various instruments with the leader playing a violin. After a break, the teacher introduced himself and engaged in conversation with the group. It wasn't long before he found out the person he was looking for was not there. He pulled out his card, handing it to the violin player and asked if he would pass it on to Israel. "Just tell him someone from Peabody Institute was looking for him, and ask him to give me a call, please."

"Will do," answered the musician.

The following week when Israel returned, the first order of business was giving Israel the business card of the Peabody teacher. Israel asked, "Do you know what he wanted?"

"I think to offer you a scholarship to Peabody," he answered. "Peabody? Peabody? You mean that great music school up on Mount Vernon Place?" Israel asked.

Israel made the call. The teacher explained how he'd heard about Israel and his violin and wanted to audition him for a possible scholarship to the elite school. Israel, not knowing much about the historic school, asked many questions. After he got the answers, they set a date when to meet and closest friends were invited. On a given night in room 100, the small group of musicians did not practice, everyone was seated waiting for the audition to start. The teacher gave the signal and Israel started to warm up. The warm up itself was masterful. The teacher thought, I like what I see.

Then the violin music started. After three different melodies were completed, the teacher quietly asked, "When can I speak to your parents?" Israel wondered how he had done but didn't ask. His phone number was given, everyone shook hands and the teacher left. Within three days the teacher was visiting the Turow home.

"Mr. and Mrs. Turow, the other night I had the privilege of hearing your son play the violin. The young man is an extraordinary, absolutely marvelous musician. Whoever his teacher is, they're doing a fine job!"

Israel took a deep breath, he had his answer. "We at Peabody are a community of teachers and instructors working with talented musicians and dancers, who are passionate about the arts, and dedicated to being the best they can be. Our goal is to turn a special talent into one that is exceptional. Our reputation speaks for itself, we're considered one of the best. As Senior Administrator, I am authorized to offer your son, Israel, a two year scholarship to our institution. I also can eliminate an original audition and some other red tape. The logistics are easy, instead of coming home from school and working with a private teacher, he will now go from school to Peabody for two hours a day. Transportation is easy, number 16 streetcar on Broadway connects to number 10, which stops right in front of our building. Whole trip takes about thirty minutes. Mr. and Mrs. Turow, you don't have to make a decision this minute, I can register him anytime. The bottom line is, your son is an exceptional talent. One we see very rarely. After all, he's been playing since he was five, that's unheard of. He'll be fine no matter what you decide. But attending Peabody will polish him, teach him about the peaks and valleys that come with music and having his name associated with Peabody certainly won't hurt his resume! And guess what, it won't cost you a penny."

Israel's father and mother looked at each other and after a few seconds Jenny asked, "Israel, what do you think?"

"I'd love to, Ma, just never thought we could afford it!" The parents signed the forms and Israel started attending Peabody Institute the following Monday.

CHAPTER 22

After going to the Administration Office to sign in, (most details were already taken care of) Israel was assigned to Mrs. Van Gleason's music class. A teacher for many years, she was considered one of the best. After her initial warm greeting, she told him to have a seat in the violin section, at any open chair. There were ten violin students seated and one empty chair, where Israel sat. He quickly caught on to what the group was playing and joined in. The days went well and Israel was comfortable in the new environment. All the violin section (seven boys and three girls) were extremely friendly, especially the first chair, Michael Van Gleason. He updated Israel's books and explained the entire program, in detail. It was uncanny how much Michael knew about what was going on.

During breaks, the two boys often would get a snack together and share stories. When returning home every night at dinner, Israel enjoyed telling the family what went on that day and how much he liked the school.

It didn't take long for Israel to learn about the teacher's grading system. It was all about where you sat, it was all about the chairs. When not leading in the front of the room, the teacher would walk between the students, listening to their pitch, tempo, and all around sound, then make mental notes to herself. She would then follow that up with adjustments to their seating. The better musicians, the closer to the front they sat. After two weeks, the teacher made an announcement. "The following students will move to the designated seats: Miss Albury, seat number eleven. Mr. Goldstein, seat number ten. Miss Jacobs, seat number six. Mr. Turow, seat number two. Everyone else, please remain where you are."

Israel was thrilled to move up. Number one seat Michael, smiled, stood up, and shook Israel's hand. This seat change happened every four weeks. The names varied but Van Gleason and Turow remained the same for six months. Unexpectedly, one Friday, the teacher announced, "Since it's the weekend and you've all been working very hard, after lunch, instead of the normal practice, you're all going to relax and be judges to the Van Gleason-Turow Violin Playoff!" Everyone stood up and clapped, they'd had a feeling this was going to happen sometime.

Michael and Israel stood up and hugged, patting each other on the back. "It's 11:45, if you're going out to lunch, be back here one PM sharp!" said the teacher firmly. Most of the students left the room, including Michael and Israel, who generally ate together.

At one PM, the room filled with excitement and people backslapping the two combatants for good luck. When everyone was seated, the teacher announced, "We will flip a coin, deciding who chooses to go first. The music will be 'The Violin Sonata Number 3', which everyone is familiar with, and no time limit. However, if you stop for any reason, you're done!" The boys nodded and the teacher flipped the coin. The boys shouted their choices. "Tails!" shouted Michael. The coin was tails and Michael chose to be first.

The music started. Michael played beautifully. There was no question about his talent. When finished, silence, then a burst of applause. Israel knew he had quite a challenge but he was ready, somehow competition never really bothered him. Israel shook Michael's hand and then he started to play. Teacher and students listened admirably as the violin music filled the room. So soft, so tender, so beautiful. Then POP! A broken string! Without any hesitation, Israel quickly changed keys, avoiding the use of the broken string, done so quickly and artistically that many in the room were not aware of the issue, they just thought it was part of the music.

However, Mrs. Van Gleason and Michael knew and admired his skill. When all was completed and the students settled down, the teacher asked for a show of hands as she called out each contestant. Out of nine students voting, excluding Michael and Israel, the vote was five to four in favor of Michael. Israel wondered how he even got four votes. He knew Michael's finished product was the better music.

Israel felt good about what he had accomplished. Considering what had happened, he knew he had done well. As the class cleared out for the weekend, the teacher called Israel aside saying, "We both know what happened. I'm very proud of you, young man! Most students would have stopped and asked for a start over but not you, not Israel Turow!"

Israel smiled and said, "Thanks, Mrs. Van, I appreciate that!"

Two days later, Michael Van Gleason approached the teacher after class and asked, "Mrs. Van, may I respectfully make a request?"

"Certainly Mr. Van what is your request?" Even though Mrs. Van was Michael's mom, he still called her Mrs. Van during school.

"We both know what happened to Israel, how he switched keys and everything, he was amazing. We also both know he is the better musician. I am requesting that Israel Turow move into the first chair."

The teacher looked at her son admiringly and said,

"I shall take your request under advisement."

The boy kissed his mother on the cheek and they both left the room. Three days later Israel Turow was seated in the first chair. In the following two years of Israel's stay at the Peabody Institute, he never relinquished that spot.

CHAPTER 23

When Israel reached age twelve, his schedule got a little hectic. First, there was regular school, then commuting to and attending Peabody Conservatory and now, Bar Mitzvah lessons had to be added. In approximately twelve months, according to the Jewish religion, Israel would become a man. The exact date was determined by the readings he was given to chant from the Torah. These are called his Maftir and Haftorah, which his teacher assigned to him, trying to reach the closest Saturday to his actual birthday. His teacher was Hazzan Weinberg at the Eden Street Synagogue. A Hazzan is a Cantor with many years of experience and in time becomes a Hazzan. Hazzan Weinberg directed liturgical prayer and lead the chanting of the prayers at the synagogue. He also taught music to both children and adults, like Bar Mitzvah lessons. The Hazzan also worked closely with the Rabbi, who conducted the service.

After discussions with parents, the Hazzan, and Peabody teacher Mrs. Van Gleason, it was decided that Israel would skip Peabody on Wednesday, which was only a half a day anyway, and go to two sessions to

Hebrew school that day. This would be two hours in the morning, have lunch, and come back two hours in the afternoon. Also added was two hours on Sunday mornings. This gave the boy three Bar Mitzvah lessons a week, which the Hazzan felt was adequate. If he fell behind, more time could be added later.

Hazzan Weinberg was a stately gentleman with a small beard, he walked with a cane, and had a slight Yiddish accent. Israel found him pleasant at their first meeting. In the class were four other boys, each learning his particular Maftir and Haftorah, plus the general Bruches that everyone chanted. Israel was assigned his special passages. Each day and each week, he was feeling more comfortable and moving along nicely. It was common practice for the Hazzan to tap his cane on the table top if someone made a mistake. One day, after a mistake by one of the boys, the Hazzan cracked his cane on the table very hard, scaring everyone out of their wits! Everyone jumped, Israel fell off the chair. Everyone laughed, the Hazzan was hysterical.

Israel did it to be funny and the Hazzan understood his humor.

After class, Israel was called aside by the teacher. "I hear you play the violin?" Hazzan asked.

"Yes sir" came the answer.

"Alright, young man, here's the deal... if you and the boys continue working hard with your lessons, I'll let you play for the group once a month!" declared the teacher.

"Fine with me!" came the answer. Thereafter, the last class of every month, the Hazzan devoted to Israel playing the violin. Everyone was happy, everyone worked harder. The twelve months flew by and Israel had his Bar Mitzvah. Because he read music so well from the violin, it helped with his chanting of the Prayers. His voice was clear and mellow and each note on perfect pitch. He chanted the Maftir and Haftorah beautifully. After the service, the congregation was invited to a luncheon (Kiddush) downstairs.

That evening, the family had an open house for family and friends. Israel's closest friends were invited, that included Arnie Hartman, Sol Gerber, Luki Savage and three girls, Julie, Rhey, and Bibi Benesh. During the festivities, Israel was asked to play the violin. He obliged. While playing, the photographer captured a picture of Israel in his spanking new Bar Mitzvah suit, brown tweed knickers with high stockings and belted jacket, holding his violin. This picture was always special to Israel. He felt it truly showed who he was.

CHAPTER 24

Every year, between January and February, music brochures from around the world would come across Mrs. Van Gleason's desk. Most were too far away or of little interest to the Peabody professor and wound up in the trash. One brochure she always looked for was the camp brochure from Juilliard School of Music in New York City. Besides their world renowned, prestigious year-round school of music, voice, dance, and acting, they also had a Summer Camp program available for one or two months or for the whole summer. The students were housed in college dormitories, ate in college cafeterias, and went to classes just a few blocks away. The special thing about the camp, if the student so chose, was that they could stay with one program all month or go to various programs, giving them a little taste of everything during their stay. Tuition for camp was average, except in the rare cases where a scholarship might be offered. Peabody Institute had a long running association with Juilliard, where they offered a one month camp scholarship each summer to the most deserving student, but not necessarily the most talented. Sometimes they were both. So, it was Mrs. Van Gleason's delight to make this offer to someone special in her class. She had a month to make the decision.

Several weeks later, during class, a messenger came into the room, handing the teacher a note. She was wanted in the office for a few minutes. She bent over and whispered to Israel, "I have to go to the office for a few minutes... maybe fifteen or twenty, will you keep them busy for me?"

"Yes, Mam," answered Israel. For five minutes or so, each student worked on their own. Then Israel got up on the podium and announced, "Got an idea... let's all turn to page twenty-one, 'The Nocturne', since we all know it pretty well, let's try playing it together, like one orchestra. It should be fun! Follow my lead... one, two, three, four." Most started together. After a few bars, Israel stopped the group and made a few friendly corrections.

Everyone was pleasantly surprised at the leader's knowledge and followed his instructions. He also explained, "Besides my hands, also watch my face and body, they also are saying something!"

They started again, this time, all together. They sounded good... pretty damn good! Mrs. Van came down the hall and as she approached the door, she heard the music. Instead of opening the door, she peaked through the window, watched and listened. 'I'll be damned,' she thought, 'this kid is special, very special!' She walked in, said nothing, and just thanked Israel for watching the class. When the period was over and most students had left, the teacher called Israel to her desk. "Young man, I was listening and saw what you did!" she bellowed.

Oh shit, he thought, I'm in trouble now. "Before you blame the class, Ms.Van, it was my doing, my idea!"

She answered, "I know whose idea it was and I can only say, it was fantastic, they sounded great! In my twenty years teaching here at Peabody, you may be the most gifted student I have ever had."

He blushed, he was relieved. "Thank you Ms. Van," he whispered. "Where did you learn to lead?" asked the teacher.

"Oh, just something I picked up from playing the violin," said Israel.

She answered, "Well, young man, I have a little reward for you, if you get your parents okay. I have a one month scholarship to give to Juilliard School of Music in New York, includes room, board, classes, and round trip transportation. And what's great about the Juilliard Camp, you can go to any class you want, any day... music, voice, dancing, or acting. You can get a little feel for everything or just stay in the violin class. One thing I know you'll love is meeting and working with Maestro Eric Galliano, one of the Board of Directors, who teaches conducting two days a week at camp. He's the well-known conductor of the New Yorker Symphony Orchestra and he's one of the best! If your parents say yes, have them fill out the enclosed forms and return everything to me, okay?"

With mouth open, Israel was stunned. "Thank you Ms. Van, thank you very much!" he answered warmly.

Israel and parents had a long discussion. It was decided he would attend Juilliard Summer Camp.

CHAPTER 25

On a beautiful Sunday morning, the train to New York brought back pleasant memories. It seemed like yesterday he was riding this same train heading to Baltimore after arriving from Russia. He was fourteen years old now, almost ready for high school. How time flies!

The information letter from the Juilliard Camp told him to report to the main auditorium, which he easily found. He was warmly greeted, given a box lunch, drink, and dessert. The campers then registered and were assigned room numbers. After checking the room, unpacking a few things, everyone was to report back to the auditorium for orientation. All the rules and regulations were announced and the faculty was introduced. Each got a warm applause. The famous Symphony Orchestra Conductor, Maestro Eric Galliano, the one Mrs. Van had told Israel about, received a rousing applause when introduced.

When the meeting was over, students were told to have dinner, relax, and be ready for classes of their choice at nine AM. Breakfast was at seven AM. Israel was excited! As the days went on, Israel spent a half a day a week in voice, where he learned to create head tones. Israel always had a pleasant voice. His knowledge of music helped him. Adding head tones gave him the ability to reach higher notes. He was pleased with his progress in voice.

The second half a day a week went to acting, where he learned how to put himself into a role before delivering the lines. This made a big change in reading a script. He enjoyed seeing the difference this made in playing a part. The second full day a week went to conducting with Maestro Eric Galliano. This was very exciting.

One day, Israel had the privilege of playing the violin for this special teacher. Galliano was impressed. Maestro was not only an excellent teacher, but exciting to be around, as he explained the various concepts of conducting. Most importantly, Israel learned how a musician in an orchestra must read the conductor's face and body as well as the movement of his hands. Being a leader of any type of orchestra, you must know how to apply all three.

Israel loved this class. Someday he hoped to lead his own orchestra.

The other three full days of the week were spent in the violin class, where he worked with Professor Marvin Silverman. The teacher knew music and he really knew the violin. As much as Israel thought he already knew about the violin, this teacher taught him so much more. Also, Silverman was extremely warm, almost like he had met Israel before. Besides teaching at Juilliard, the professor was also the first chair violinist with Maestro's Symphony Orchestra. He was a very busy man. Unknown to Israel, Silverman also knew Van Gleason from the many Peabody scholarships she'd sent him through the years. They spoke on the telephone occasionally and when they did, Israel Turow's name often came up.

Professor Silverman recognized Israel the moment he walked in the door but said nothing. The camp was only thirty days long and the four weeks flew by. The last day was bittersweet. Camp was over and time to go home. Handshakes and hugs were abound to friends and teachers to be missed.

As Professor Silverman said his goodbyes to the class, he asked Israel to stay a moment. Israel wondered what he had done wrong.

"Well, what did you think of camp?" he asked.

"Mr. Silverman, this whole setup at Juilliard is fantastic, even though it's a learning experience like school... they make it fun. I wish I could stay here the whole summer!"

The teacher asked, "How would you like to go to

Juilliard all year?"

"Would love it but know my parents couldn't afford it," replied Israel.

"How about if you got a scholarship from Juilliard, would you still love it?" quizzed the teacher.

"Would I... are you joking, Mr. Silverman, are you joking sir?"

"No, I think I can swing it, a year from now. What grade are you in school?" he asked.

"I start high school next month, sir." said Israel.

Silverman replied, "That means you'll finish up Peabody a year from now, right?"

"That's right, sir, but how did you know about me and Peabody?"

"Oh, I know all about you from Mrs. Van Gleason, she sends me scholarships every year!"

Israel couldn't help but ask excitedly, "You mean you knew all about me before I walked into class?"

"Absolutely," answered the teacher. He told Israel he would stay in touch with him and Mrs. Van all year and if all was well, he'd send scholarship forms to his parents next summer.

"Have a good year!" the teacher said as he shook Israel's hand.

CHAPTER 26

Israel and his friends were now in their first year of high school. His after-school two years at the Peabody Institute was now completed. After school was now devoted to violin practice or school activities.

Paterson Park Senior High School had served the East Baltimore corridor for many years. Students have excelled in academics, athletics, and the arts. Its faculty was considered one of the best in the Baltimore area. One reason for this was a veteran teacher by the name of Barbara Bennett. Mrs. Bennett headed the music department, which included glee club, orchestra and musical productions. The teacher was well versed in all phases of music and beloved by her vast ensemble of former students who often came back to visit. After a week or so, both Barbara Bennett and the students got acclimated to each other. The students found out they had a very savvy leader in Mrs. Bennett. She was warm and friendly and most important, fair to everyone. The teacher learned she had some very good voices in the glee club, especially a fine tenor and a new soprano who had a beautiful voice. The teacher was hoping that both would audition for the Spring Operetta.

In the Orchestra, she found a new violist, who played the instrument like a veteran, as if he had taken lessons for years. He was just starting high school, when could he have started?

As the months rolled on, glee club and orchestra were singing and playing contemporary songs and music, a little bit of everything. By mid-January, the teacher announced the name and date of the Spring Operetta. It was entitled *Eileen*, a comic operetta, with music by Victor Herbert, lyrics and book by Henry Blossom. The performances were scheduled for the weekends of May tenth and seventeenth and auditions would be the week of February tenth. Barbara Bennett picked this particular musical mainly because of its very fine score. The overall songs were good but the main ballad, a love song entitled 'Thine Alone' was considered one of Victor Herbert's and Henry Blossom's finest works. The teacher knew the right soprano and tenor voices could really do justice to this special melody.

Bennett's musicals were always a "sell out" and this one would follow the trend.

Since the glee club fed the show's cast and chorus and the orchestra played the show's performances, after tryouts, everything was now concentrated on the musical. The glee club was now singing all of the show's songs and the orchestra was now working on the score. Auditions had a good turnout and all parts were filled. The lead tenor, who was expected, did come out and got the part. There was almost a tie for the lead soprano. The lead soprano Bennett as expected did come out, but so did another girl with quite a bit of talent. Her delivery of the lines was better, her movement on the stage was better and her voice was good. The only problem, instead of being a soprano, which the *labrado* called for, she was a mezzo-soprano, a slightly lower voice. This would entail the key being changed and possibly losing some of the fullness and richness of the music. It was decided to give the part to the soprano. The teacher didn't want to leave herself short in case of an emergency, so she asked the other girl to be the understudy.

Her name was Julia Benesh.

CHAPTER 27

Rehearsals were going well. After four weeks most of the principals could put their books down and deliver the lines from memory. Everything started to mesh together. The two leads', Arnold Singer, tenor and Farlene Sable, soprano, voices blended together nicely. Occasionally, when things got a little out of sorts, Bennett called for extra rehearsals, until they got it right. Because of this, there was little time for the understudies to receive any work. Julia Benesh was in the chorus and working hard. She also took her understudy role very seriously. One day, the female lead was late and Julia jumped right in and did surprisingly well. They hadn't gotten to the heavy singing yet so she really wasn't tested, but Julia knew the lines and blocking well. She also gained a lot of confidence after this episode. The teacher was extremely pleased that Julia was ready, without warning. She let the cast know how important an understudy could be. Now, Julia really knew she was going to be ready if ever needed again.

Several times a week, after dinner in a quiet space, Julia would practice by herself. For a while, she was getting comfortable doing this, but soon she realized without the music and songs, it was pretty much a waste of time. She needed help. Wait a minute! Israel Turow, whom she saw a little bit and liked, knew all the music, he played it every day at rehearsal!

Maybe... just maybe? When asked, Israel was glad to oblige. They agreed to meet at each other's houses, depending which one was the quietest on a given night. At their first get-together, Julia was surprised how much of the show Israel had memorized. Except for a few places, where he paraphrased, he could almost do the entire show from memory, lines and blocking. Israel could also do the songs but could not reach the high notes properly, even with the head tones. It was decided that he would substitute the violin for the male lead, just giving Julia a nod when he was doing so. It worked out. He played her part with her and then with a head- nod, played the male-lead's part.

As Israel did this, Julia could envision the male singer performing, thus she was able to concentrate on her proper blocking. After repeated violin practices, with the usual key lowered for Julia, Israel noticed, without too much effort, she was almost hitting the higher notes like that of the soprano. One practice, without telling Julia, Israel played the music in the higher key, as written. Julia went through the song hitting all the notes perfectly. When finished, she knew she did something different. "What happened?" she asked.

Israel explained, "I played it in a higher key. Because of the repeated practice with the violin, which gives a very clear human voice like sound, your brain, without warning, just took you up to the higher key. To be truthful, I thought you sounded fine!" Also, without knowing it, some of the family had peeked from another room when they heard the new soprano voice. "Sounds very good," they commented.

Julia was delighted. She thought, how great it was having Israel around to help her. Now, if she needed to jump in they won't have to change the key! Israel was very happy to practice with Julia. He liked the ending the most. That's when the male lead would put the violin down and kiss the female lead.

One day, after a long rehearsal where Julia replaced the female lead due to sickness, the teacher told Julia, "If auditions were being held now, Julia would be the female lead." Julia was ecstatic over the compliment but quickly explained how much Israel Turow knew about the musical and had helped her. The teacher was surprised and not been aware of Israel's talent beyond the violin. She suggested to Julia to "continue whatever they had been doing, because it's working fine!"

CHAPTER 28

Israel was working a hectic schedule. He had regular school, orchestra practice, musical rehearsals and worked several evenings a week with Julia on the Operetta. But no matter what, he still practiced with his violin, either early in the morning, middle afternoon, or late in the evening. He always got in his two hours of violin practice.

One day during school, Julia received a note to please see Professor Bennett when convenient. By coincidence, Israel got the same note. When speaking about it, they both decided to see the teacher together. During a break in classes, they visited the music teacher. She greeted them warmly and explained nothing was wrong, she just had an update for Julia. Since they had been working together, she thought it best to speak to both of them. The teacher said, "Farlene's mother called and informed the teacher that Mr. Sable, Farlene's father, was having major heart surgery on Friday May ninth, and that Farlene would have to miss the dress rehearsal that evening. Hopefully, Farlene will be ready for opening night."

This meant Julia had to be the lead soprano Friday

night and possibly Saturday if Farlene couldn't make it. The teacher assured Julia not to worry because she had been doing a good job at rehearsals. Julia looked at Israel quizzically.

"Rehearsals are one thing, we're now talking about being the real lead!" Israel looked at Julia and convincingly said, "Julia, don't worry, you're going to be okay. We'll work that much harder!"

The teacher smiled and agreed. She waved goodbye and said, "See you later at rehearsal!"

Now, Mrs. Bennett had Julia rehearse directly with Arnold Singer, the tenor, at least once a week. Julia and Israel continued working together several evenings a week. The pace increased and Julia was getting more confident and singing much more relaxed. However, during Tech Week, Julia noticed during rehearsals, Arnold Singer sometimes carried an inhaler with him.

She wondered what that was about. She asked Israel to check. He found out Arnold had a slight case of asthma but it didn't affect his singing, since he used the inhaler ahead of time, if needed. As the weeks grew closer to dress rehearsal, Bennett was having Julia play the lead soprano every other day. Julia was ready!

The day of the dress rehearsal, Mrs. Bennett informed Julia there was quite a crowd expected. This made Julia both excited and a little nervous.

Everything in the green room behind the stage was ready and the cast was all set. A little earlier, the orchestra did some run throughs and they were ready also. Israel took a minute to find Julia backstage and wished her well. The lights dimmed, and the orchestra started the Overture. It was dead silent backstage, except for someone coughing in the back room. The Overture was over and the curtain rose. Everyone was in place for the opening musical number.

The dialogue started and the tenor and soprano with the chorus were in the queue. Midway through the first act, a scene ended and the next scene was to be the love song 'Thine Alone', featuring the tenor and Julia. The curtain opened, Julia in place, waiting for Arnold to appear. The orchestra played the introduction for the male lead, who was still missing. Julia was confused and completely numb. The teacher knew something was wrong. She quietly halted the orchestra and gave them the signal to start over. The orchestra started the introduction again. By this time, Israel had noticed something was wrong because Arnold was not on stage. Mrs. Bennett was about to signal the music to stop but before she did, she noticed Israel slide out of his chair.

He looked up and give a head nod to Julia. Mrs. Bennett had the orchestra continue playing a little softer. She thought she knew what Israel was going to do. Israel started the tenor's music on the violin and the chorus came in on queue and Julia was back in sync. She sang her parts perfectly. Throughout the song, facing the stage at the footlights, Israel continued playing the male parts on the violin. Julia and the chorus now knew exactly when to come in and the orchestra was now back on track. The first act finished perfectly and everyone was relieved. Arnold Singer, the tenor, after stopping a coughing spell, came back and completed the show. At the curtain call, the cast insisted that Israel Turow join them on stage. Israel hopped on stage, joined the bows, then headed for Julia. At the end, the two leads were supposed to embrace, but Arnold could not. Israel obliged. He hugged Julia and kissed her on the lips. A very long kiss! Mrs. Bennett smiled. The dress rehearsal was over. The two weekend runs went very well and played to full houses.

The Spring Musical was considered a roaring success!

CHAPTER 29

Professor Marvin Silverman from Juilliard School of Music in New York, kept his word. Every month or two, he would send scholarship information to the Turows. This included housing information, meal plans, curricula choice, health plans, and signature forms. He occasionally followed up with a phone call to assure all was ready. It looked like Israel was all set with his Juilliard Scholarship.

On the second Monday of every month, the Juilliard School had their Board of Directors meeting.

One meeting, the Board President opened the meeting with the following announcement: "The city has finally come through with our remodeling plan for our North Dormitory. The money has been appropriated in the city's budget now, if we let them start the end of the present term. They've been putting us off for five years and if we don't move immediately, we could lose this chance for another five years. The Executive Committee has decided to let the work start next month. This means next term, we lose six rooms, to be more exact, twelve scholarships. So, the only fair way to handle this is to remove the last twelve that signed up."

There was rumbling in the room as hands went up. The President said, "Since most of you have comments to make, we'll just go right around the room."

Each member spoke his piece. When it came to Marvin Silverman, he was ecstatic. "All year we've been working and promising these kids a scholarship, it just doesn't seem right, just because the budget is short of a little money."

The President answered, "Marv, it's not the money, we've got enough money to give twice the number of scholarships. It's the beds. After giving up the rooms, there's not one bed left."

Silverman answered, "You're saying, if a kid had a place to sleep, he's still got a scholarship?"

"You got it!" was the answer.

The meeting shortly ended.

One evening after dinner, the phone rang at the Turow household. Marvin Silverman wanted to speak to Israel and his parents. Mother Jenny got on one phone and Israel was on the extension. Carefully, Silverman explained the dormitory problem. And then said, "It's' only for the first year. The following year, you're all set with housing. But I vaguely remember when you were at Juilliard Camp, you once mentioned you had a relative... a sister… that lived in New York City. Is she still living there?"

"Yes, answered Israel, Ma, what do you think?"

"I'll call her. May I call you right back, Mr. Silverman?" Jenny replied. "Yes, definitely, call me collect as soon as you can." answered the teacher.

Five minutes later, Jenny had made the call. Sophie and her husband would be thrilled to have Israel stay with them. She had an extra room (her knitting room) and he could stay as long as he wanted. Jenny called Silverman back. Soon, Israel was signed up for his scholarship to the Juilliard School of Music. He would finish his last two years of high school at Juilliard. He would hone his craft and deepen his artistry.

The New York school, being a world leader in music, was where Israel would fulfill his dream of playing the violin to a different level.

CHAPTER 30

The last week in August, Israel packed his bags, said so-long to family and friends, and Julia, and headed to New York to live with sister Sophie and husband Mort. He returned to Baltimore once a month to see family and friends, and Julia. He would attend The Juilliard School of Music, the best of the best! The school was founded in 1908. Its mission was to provide the highest caliber of music and artistic education to gifted musicians and other forms of the arts, from around the world.

Israel checked into Administration and received his class schedule and list of teachers. He was thrilled to find out his violin class was headed by one of his favorites, Marvin Silverman, his scholarship benefactor and he would again study conducting under Maestro Eric Galliano. However, there were a few different teachers scattered into the schedule to broaden the learning process of other string instruments. Besides violin, Israel would also learn to play the viola, guitar, cello, banjo, harp, ukulele, and a tiny bit of piano. This was because the piano sometimes related to certain classical violin music.

The first time in class, Israel received a very warm greeting from both Silverman and Maestro. Israel was excited and looking forward to the new journey.

Sister Sophie and Husband Morton had changed the sewing room to a second bedroom. It had everything Israel needed. As the weeks went on, Israel took most of his meals at the school's cafeteria, depending on his classes. He was always welcome to join Sophie and Mort at any meal he chose or just grab something on his own. Classes were Monday through Friday.

Generally, Saturday was an off day, spending some time with sister and brother-in-law. Sunday he slept late, read The New York Times and practiced with the violin. He called home several times a week (also Julia). That schedule kept him fresh for Monday classes.

One Saturday morning Sophie approached and asked, "Izzy, do you have any plans for today? Mort's working and I'm completely free."

"Anything you want to do is okay with me," he answered.

Sophie continued, "Let's go sight-seeing around New York... you've never been to Time Square, Central Park, the Empire State Building... places like that!"

"Fine," answered Israel, "by the way... have you ever been to Carnegie Hall? I hear it's really something to see!""

"No, but we'll add it to the list... I know where it is," she answered.

They hurried off to see New York. They climbed the steps to the top of the Empire State Building. What a beautiful view! They took a stroll in Central Park, so scenic and restful. They grabbed some lunch around Time Square and shared the biggest sandwich he'd ever seen. At three-thirty, there was still plenty of the day left, so they headed for the Great Hall. They approached the building, came up to the front door. There was a large sign;

CLOSED TODAY. REHEARSAL FOR TONIGHT'S SYMPHONY WITH MAESTRO ERIC GALLIANO.

Sophie yelled, "Damn it! Just our luck we'd pick a day with a rehearsal."

Israel answered, "Hold it Soph, I've got an idea. ......"

CHAPTER 31

Israel backed away from the front of the building and looked up a side street. There he saw someone leave the building, apparently from the stage door. "Follow me Soph," he said. They both approached the door and found it unlocked. They entered, went up a few steps and saw a man sitting at a desk smoking a cigar and reading a paper. He looked up and barked, "Nobody is allowed in here today... we're having rehearsal!"

Israel said, "Excuse me sir, sorry, didn't know... we're just looking around, never been inside... this is my sister Sophie.. .I'm Israel Turow, a student of Maestro.

The man replied, "Did you say a student of Maestro?" "Yes Sir," Israel answered.

"That's different. I'm Clarence. I'm sure Maestro wouldn't mind your peeking in, just keep it quiet!"

"Absolutely, sir," they both answered.

Clarence led the way through a dark hallway and then opened a door that led them into an enormous hall. They were now inside Carnegie Hall, one of the most prestigious venues in the world for music. Its construction began in 1889. Official opening night was May 5, 1896. Originally known simply as "The Great Hall." The hall was renamed 'Carnegie Hall' in 1898.

The enormously high hall has five levels with 2,804 seats. Visitors going to the top balcony must climb one-hundred and twenty-five steps.

Israel and Sophie walked down a few rows and slipped into the seats. They heard the leader say, "Take a five minute break!" He lifted up a glass to take a drink of water. As the Leader turned from a distance, he saw two people in the audience. He shouted, "I'm sorry folks, we're closed today...we're having—"

Israel shouted back, "Maestro, it's Israel Turow, I'm here with my sister Sophie!"

The Leader replied, "Israel? What in the world are you doing here? Come, move down here so I can hear you!"

Brother and sister moved down to the first row. They explained the whole situation to Maestro. He laughed and said, "Clarence did the right thing in bringing you in, you're welcome here anytime! That goes for you too, Sophie!" Brother and sister felt a lot better.

"So, while I have a little break, tell me Israel, how

are you getting along at Juilliard?"

The reply was, "Maestro, to be perfectly frank, I don't know how they do it, how everything is so organized, everything is like clockwork, I really enjoy the way the teachers present something new almost every day. Frankly, I love the place!"

Maestro smiled and said, "You scared me for a minute. I'm glad it's working out but to be truthful, I already knew how you were doing. I often speak to various teachers, they're very happy with your progress, especially Professor Marvin Silverman."

"Yes, he's great!" said Israel.

Maestro asked, "How are you doing in conducting class?"

Israel was confused by the question and answered, "But that's your class, sir..."

"I know, but how do you think you're doing? I mean in an emergency, if you had to, could you lead an orchestra?" the Maestro asked.

Israel, not really thinking before he answered said, "Oh, yes sir, I think so!"

Maestro replied, "Well, let's see... come up here Israel!"

"What?!" screamed Israel, "What did you say?"

"I said come up here, to the podium, Israel."

CHAPTER 32

Sheepishly, and scared to death, Israel headed to the podium. The Maestro spoke to the orchestra. "Everyone turn to page twenty, 'The Nocturne', we all know it, even young Israel here. Israel, you remember this from class, right?"

Israel answered, "Yes sir!"

The Maestro spoke again to his people, "For just a few minutes, help me with a little experiment, we'll get back to rehearsal very shortly, Israel. Come up here and take this baton. Don't be nervous, pretend these people are just like your classmates... you lead them the same way... except these people are the best damned musicians in the entire world!" The entire orchestra laughed and Maestro added a big smile. The humor made Israel feel a little more relaxed.

"Israel, I want you to lead this Symphony Orchestra. Everyone knows the music, so start when you're ready."

Extremely nervous, Israel raised the baton, and counted out loud, "One, two, three."

The Maestro interrupted, "Israel, with a professional

orchestra, there is no vocal sound. It's all done with your baton, hands, face, and body. So let's begin again, don't worry, they'll all begin on your signal."

Israel tapped his baton on the stand, lifted his arms and moved the baton. Oh, my God, they all started together, Israel thought. As he progresses, he finds he is leading them, not the other way around. Since he knows the music, he signals when each instrument group comes in and how loud or soft they should play.

He truly is leading the group and becoming more and more comfortable. His facial expressions and body language is perfectly in sync. At one place in the music, the symbols in the orchestra's sheet music were different from the symbols in his classroom sheet music, which he is used to. An audience would never know the difference, but Maestro knew, Israel knew, and the orchestra knew. What will he do? thought Maestro. Israel quickly made an adjustment, the orchestra followed perfectly and everything continued as normal.

One thing Israel noticed was the outstanding acoustics in this storied beautiful building. The orchestra sounded magnificent. One could tell the ending was coming up by Israel's body language. Israel brought the orchestra to a final closing and very strong finish. Israel thought he had done well, he could just feel it. Sophie stood and clapped, Maestro clapped and something Israel did not expect, the orchestra stood and clapped including the first violinist, Marvin Silverman, his violin teacher at Juilliard!

That very moment, Israel felt something he had never experienced before: the beautiful sound of the orchestra and the majesty of the entire building.

As the ovation continued, Maestro said nothing for two minutes. When all was quiet, Maestro blurted out, "These people don't clap for just anybody!" After the laugh, Maestro put his hand on Israel's shoulder and said, "Truthfully, I expected a performance from a talented young musician to be good, stop a few times for misunderstandings, make a few adjustments with the orchestra, etc. Never did I expect a performance like that! Young man, you were outstanding... when you came to the difference in interpretation, you didn't miss a beat, you were masterful in working around it and continuing along. Israel, because you did so well today, I'm going to add this performance to your classroom grade. It will help at the end of the term."

Led by Marvin Silverman, the orchestra stood up again and clapped. Maestro then yelled, "Now, will you get the hell out of here so we can rehearse!"

Israel and Sophie skirted up the aisle heading for the exit. As they passed Clarence, Israel thanked him again.

The Doorman said, "Hope you enjoyed your visit!"

Israel answered, "One day, Clarence, I'll tell you all about it!"

CHAPTER 33

On the way home, Israel and Sophie couldn't stop talking about what had happened at Carnegie Hall. When they got home, Mort was already there and both rushed to him at once, trying to tell him what had happened that afternoon.

Sophie screamed, "Mort, you won't believe!" Israel yelled, "Mort, I gotta tell you!"

Mort tried to quiet both down. "Okay, one at a time... go ahead Soph."

Sophie caught her breath and started over slowly. She told Mort the whole story. Israel filled in anything she left out. When both were done, Mort couldn't believe what he had heard.

"Unbelievable!" he shouted. "Well, this must be our lucky day... I've got something to tell you guys. I got a promotion today! Head of the department. Fifty bucks a week more, plus added benefits!"

"Great" hollered Sophie. "Congratulations," added Israel.

"Okay, we're all going out tonight to celebrate,

dinner and drinks are on me!" Sophie and Israel hugged each other, then a hug went to Mort. Mort then explained they had plenty of time and to go relax for a while. Each went to their rooms. Israel was still excited but also quite tired from the day. He laid across the bed looking at the ceiling, just thinking.

Israel was walking up a hill on a beautiful day. It seemed beautiful at first, but then he realized everything was gold... the sky... the ground... even his clothes! When he got to the top of the hill and looked over the cliff, down below were hundreds of people, dressed in gold, holding their violins ready to play. He was totally confused and wondered where he was. Then a voicespoke from somewhere up above. It was a man's voice, soft but yet very direct.

"Hello, Israel, how are you today?" the voice spoke. Israel replied, "I am fine, who is speaking?"

The voice answered, "I gave you your first violin!"

Israel's answer was, "My first violin came from my Grandfather Jacob!" The voice said, "I know your Grandfather very well!"

"Why am I here?" asked Israel.

"You're here to lead the people in playing my music," the voice answered.

The boy answered, "I have no music to guide me."

Then noticed he had a gold baton in his hand. By this time Israel was quizzical as to what the voice looked like. He turned his head towards the sky. The gold sky was so bright he could hardly see but faintly he thought he saw the image of Maestro Galliano.

"When do I start?" asked Israel.

The voice answered, "I will tell you when to start, when to go softer, when to play louder and when to stop!"

"I am ready," spoke the boy.

"Lift your baton and start now!" the voice said.

Israel lifted his baton and started. Everyone began playing. As he continued, the melody was familiar, he knew what he was playing. The voice said, "lower," Israel obeyed. Moments later, the voice said, "softer," Israel obeyed. Finally, the voice said, "stop." Israel gave an ending motion and all stopped, all together.

The voice said, "You did well Israel, very well. Because of that, I have something for you!"

Quizzically, Israel asked, "What might that be?" A hand came out of the sky and touched Israel's left shoulder. The touch was so soft, like a feather. But he did feel the touch.

"Who are you, what is your name?" questioned the boy. "It's Time, it's Time…" came the answer.

As it became softer, it then became louder, "IT'S TIME, IT'S TIME…"

"Izzy, wake up, IT'S TIME to clean up, we're leaving in fifteen minutes!"

Israel opened his eyes, sat up in the bed and saw Mort in the doorway. "Oh my gosh, it was a dream, but it seemed so real!" yelled Israel.

Mort spoke back, "What are you talking about? Whatever, get ready, we're leaving soon!"

Israel got ready and the three took off. The celebratory dinner was a thick steak smothered in onions, baked potato, green beans, and two mugs of beer. Everyone was feeling good. Israel felt especially good, better than he'd felt in a long time. But the touch?

It had felt so real.

CHAPTER 34

The days grew into weeks, weeks to months and somehow, two years flew by. Israel graduated Juilliard at the top of his class. His antennas were always up, listening to how to improve every day. When leaving, it was a sad day having to say goodbye to so many friends and teachers. When giving his opinion about the school, Israel commented, "I will never forget the wonderful training I have received at Juilliard, the finest school in the world for teaching of the Arts." He now was ready for the music world, thanks to that fantastic school.

After hugs and kisses and a tremendous feel of gratitude to Sophie and Mort, Israel headed back home to Baltimore. The family (and a special young lady) quickly noticed, when they sent their son off to New York, he was a boy. He returned as a man. Israel returned to his daily routine of practice, practice, practice. But now, he included letters and calls to fellow musicians around the East Coast. Would they be interested in moving to Baltimore? He wanted to form his own orchestra.

After being schooled in playing many instruments, he now knew what to look for in the different sounds that he wanted. Interviewing one at a time, he built up the group to twelve. He wanted three more to act as alternates. The orchestra got together weekly for practice. When he felt they were ready, he and his new business manager, Arnold Hartman, placed ads in *The Jewish Times* and *Baltimore Sun*, looking for Bar Mitzvah and wedding customers. The business came rather quickly and before he realized it, he was booked pretty far in advance. The name 'The Israel Turow Orchestra' became quite popular around the Baltimore area. Business was good and Israel was able to put some money away.

While he was building his business, he never forgot where his heart lied. Israel and Julia were seeing a lot of each other. They had become a real item. Often, she would accompany him to wedding and Bar Mitzvah engagements. One day, Israel proposed to Julia. She answered, "Yes! I do love you, but we have to get Papa's permission!" Israel agreed. Julia set up an appointment for Israel and Father to meet.

Israel was extremely nervous, but bravely asked the father for his daughter's hand. Papa Benesh smiled, looked Israel in the eyes and asked, "How much money do you have in the bank?"

Israel answered, "Five hundred and sixty dollars!"

"That's good," answered the father. "I know you two love each other and that's very important. I approve of you, so here's the deal... when you have one thousand in the bank, we'll have a wedding!"

Israel agreed and they both shook hands. Julia and Israel were engaged!

CHAPTER 35

In 1921, the Century Theatre opened on Lexington and Charles Streets in Baltimore. It came complete with a large ballroom above the movie house. The ballroom dancing did not work out. Five years later, the ballroom space was converted into an atmospheric style theatre called The Valencia Theatre. It opened on December 24, 1926, featuring first run silent movies. Prior to its opening, there were auditions to select an orchestra to play music during the movie's storyline.

Five different orchestras vied for The Valencia's musical contract. The Israel Turow Orchestra won the competition.

Playing weekend Bar Mitzvahs and weddings was easy. The orchestra made the rules and there was no one watching over their shoulder for the slightest deviation. The six day Valencia job was full time, Tuesday through Sunday, closed on Mondays to the general public but the orchestra had to work a few hours rehearsing future movies. Rules and regulations had to be adhered to. This was a big step for Israel and the group. It was their first full-time job. But, on the plus side, there was steady income every week, medical insurance, plus one week vacation a year with pay and ten sick days a year. They all realized it was a pretty good deal. The only issue was having enough musicians on weeks that also had bookings for Saturday and Sunday. Since weekend business was not guaranteed, there had to be extra musicians hired to cover when both venues were full. With Arnold Hartman's help the two men set up a rotating schedule, where three to four men were off on non-working weekends. That seemed to be the only fair way and the whole orchestra agreed to it. Israel and his orchestra were working steadily and everything seemed to mesh as the months rolled by.

Israel and Julia talked every evening, either by phone or in person. One night, at the Benesh home, the two were talking about many things. After an hour, Israel casually said, "Oh, by the way, I've got a thousand dollars in the bank... in fact, to be exact, it's fourteen hundred!"

Julia screamed, "When were you going to tell me, you've been here over an hour."

Nonchalantly, Israel answered, "Sometime this month."

Julia got up, went over to her fiancé, started to give him a hit when he grabbed her and gave her a kiss.

Papa Benesh walked into the room. "What's going on here?" he bellowed.

Julia told him, "Israel has something to tell you!" "Yes, young man?"

"Nothing important Pa, just something about money."

Julia screamed, "Tell him!!"

"Papa, I have fourteen hundred dollars in the bank," exclaimed Israel.

Papa smiled to answer Israel's humor and said, "I would think that's rather important."

He turned and screamed loudly, "Everyone, come in here this minute!!"

Mama and the children are all scared to death, they rushed into the living room.

Papa Benesh yelled out, "Leah, children, we're going to have a wedding!"

CHAPTER 36

Both sets of parents, Julia, and Israel, agreed to meet for dinner at their favorite East Baltimore Street Deli, Sussman and Lev. After the pickles and sauerkraut, the conversation got serious. To start with, Harry Benesh made it perfectly clear, being his first wedding, for his oldest daughter, that he and Leah were covering the total cost of the wedding; including hall, food, liquor, flowers, and whatever else Julia wanted. And there was no discussion about it.

Izik said, "Harry, we thank you for your generosity, but we want to help someway... how about we do the flowers?"

"Absolutely not!" answered Harry. "Now no further discussion about money!"

Israel spoke up. "Papa, you're being extremely generous, I have a suggestion... we'll cover the Rabbis, the rehearsal dinner, and... and... the music!"

Quickly Harry answered, "Music, music, what kind of music. I thought we'd be dancing with the radio! By the way, do you know of a decent orchestra?"

After the laughter subsided, Leah spoke up, "You

know, Julia and the girls probably will be making most of the plans, so we really don't have to do much tonight, except pick a date!"

After discussing what days the holidays fell on and other important dates of interest, the group decided on a date. Julia and Israel would be married on Sunday April 15, 1927.

As the bright clouds showed through each day and the fun of planning a wedding continued, everything was running smoothly. The hotel with food and drink was booked plus florist and photographer were reserved.

Everything was all set.

However, out west in Movieland, there was a dark cloud brewing for silent movies that few people in the East gave much thought to: the conversion of silent movies to the talkies. The transition from silent films to the talkies in the mid 1920's transformed the face of the American film industry.

Going to the picture show was a wondrous experience that for twenty-five cents gave Americans in large cities an escape from their tedious lives and offered an evening of crystal chandeliers, marble fountains, gilt, inlay and richly upholstered seats. They went to enjoy the silent movies. Without dialogue, the actors had only body language and expression to tell the story. As an intensely visual medium, the silent film was accessible to all audiences and in areas where there were large immigrant populations and English was not the first language, the intertitles would be translated into Yiddish, Russian, or Italian as the live music from the orchestra in the pit accompanied the film. The Vitaphone, endorsed by Warner Brothers, was used to make the first "hail silent-half talking" musical, *The Jazz Singer* in October 1927, which was met with great success. The Vitaphone technology recorded sound on a separate wax disc that the projectionist then had to synchronize with the film.

The response from the general public and the industry unfolded, leading to an eventual transition from silent film to talkies. It was only a matter of time before everything changed completely.

CHAPTER 37

Sunday, April 15, 1927, was a beautiful day for a wedding. Bright sunny skies, seventy-two degree temperature, light warm breezes. Standing before Rabbi Adere Cobum and Chazen Adolph Wiseman at the Eden Street synagogue was bride Julia Benesh and groom Israel Turow. On the other side, next to Israel was the best man, Arnold Hartman. Parents, Harry and Leah Benesh and Izik and Jenny Turow, stood just behind their child.

Father Harry, had just brought his daughter down the aisle, kissed her, and presented her to the groom. In the procession, brothers Leonard Benesh and Herman Turow, led the ushers. Sisters Rachel and Beatrice Benesh and Ida and Sadi Turow led the bridesmaids. The service was beautiful; both mothers cried. The couple took their vows, exchanged rings, drank the ceremonial wine, and took their blessings from the Rabbi. They kissed.

Israel closed the ceremony by breaking the glass with his foot. They were married. Mr. and Mrs. Israel Stanley Turow!

The Belvedere Hotel was a Beaux Arts style building in Baltimore, Maryland. It was designed by the Boston architectural firm of Parker and Thomas in 1902. The hotel was a Baltimore landmark at the Southeast corner of North Charles Street, facing north on East Chase Street in the city's fashionable Mount Vernon-Belvedere-Mount Royal neighborhood. It was considered one of Baltimore's best. That's what Harry Benesh wanted for his daughter Julia's wedding. The best!

It was a black-tie affair for one-hundred and twenty guests that started at 7:30 PM. The main ballroom was elegant with white and pink flowers and decorations everywhere. The party started in a Hawaiian themed side room with cocktails, hors d'oeuvres, and violin music. Gradually, everyone moved into the main hall for dinner. Everything was perfect. Wonderful food and continuous flowing wine on every table, plus an open bar for whatever else someone might want.

The music was outstanding, yet, no one knew its name. It had some stranger leading it named Arnie Hartman. The plan was a seven day honeymoon at the Grossinger's Hotel in the Borscht Belt of New York.

However, when the evening was over and the newlyweds returned to their hotel room, Israel was very tired and felt a little feverish. Even though it was two AM, Julia thought it best if she called their family Physician Dr. Hornberg. He would understand the unusual late hour call, since they were expected to leave for their honeymoon at 7 AM and needed some answers.

Dr. Hornberg said Julia had done the right thing in calling and he'd be over in twenty minutes. The doctor examined Israel and found he had 102 temperature. Also, there was a slight redness around Israel's left neck area.

Under the circumstances of the wedding and all the excitement involved, it could just be fatigue. The doctor didn't feel there was any emergency at the moment. He left Israel some medication and instructed Julia to give him plenty of liquids and water. He suggested waiting on the honeymoon for a few hours, sleep late tomorrow morning, and see how he felt.

Julia and Israel shut off the alarm clock and decided to sleep late and just rest the next day. Julia got up once to give her husband some medicine and a glass of water. She felt his head, he felt cooler. They both slept late. Israel was feeling much better, like the fever was gone.

He was hungry. They had breakfast in bed. They agreed to cancel the honeymoon temporarily and rethink it in a few weeks. They made a few calls to update everyone about their plans.

Grossinger's Hotel was very understanding, they didn't lose a penny! So, the newlyweds spent the first couple of days of their honeymoon at the Belvedere Hotel. They'd find something to do!

CHAPTER 38

After several days' rest, the two honeymooners went back to their regular routines, Israel with his orchestra and Julia with her Assistant Buyers job at Hochischild Kohn's Department Store. It was decided they would postpone their honeymoon for a few months, until their schedules permitted.

One morning, in Israel's mailbox at the Valencia Theatre, there was a note from the theatre's manager for Israel to come to the office as soon as possible.

Israel reported to the office that afternoon. Sidney Lipturitz, partner and theatre manager spoke, "Izzy, the theatre bought two weeks of *The Jazz Singer*. It starts the first of next month! As you know, it's a talkie, so no music is necessary."

Slightly shocked, but not completely, Israel replied, "So, what'll we do?"

"It looks like we have to cancel the contract. To go even further, all the movies we bought for the rest of the year, are going to be talkies. The orchestra music in the pit is over all over the country. The contract says either side can cancel with two weeks' notice. Your group has done a good job for us, so we're going to do better than that. You'll finish up the next two weeks as scheduled. We're going to give you and your entire group one month severance pay. Possibly, by the end of that time, you guys will have found something else."

Israel softly thanked the manager, shook hand, and left the office.

But there was more. Dark clouds were forming all over. Not only orchestras were canceled but thousands of other jobs were being lost all over the country due to the beginning of the Great Depression. It was the worst economic downturn in the history of the industrialized world, starting with the stock market crash of 1929. Not only was the theatre job closing, the weekend Bar Mitzva and wedding parties were drastically off due to the decline of lavish affairs.

One evening after dinner, Julia asked Israel to sit down, she wanted to talk to him. A little worried, Israel sat, looked into her eyes and said, "What's wrong, sweetheart? Please don't worry, everything is going to work out."

She looked at him, smiling and said, "I'm not worried Izzy, it's just that I have something to tell you... you're going to be a father at the end of November!"

Israel was surprised and relieved. He thought something was wrong, he was nervous. "Are you sure? How do you know?" He grabbed Julia and kissed her.

"Women always know, silly," she said.

He jumped for joy, he was excited... really excited! "Can the doctor tell what it is yet?" he questioned.

"No, we won't know until the baby is born, so we have to start picking names for both!" she answered.

"Okay, late November, we have plenty of time, when can we tell the family?" he asked.

"Right now!"

CHAPTER 39

They agreed on one thing. The baby's name would start with an M. It would be named after his brother Morris. Not knowing boy or girl, they went through names, over and over. But it was only July, so they had plenty of time. After a while, it seemed like he was working on boys' names and she was doing the girls' names. She had all the normal signs of pregnancy, stomach was getting bigger and bigger and the occasional morning sickness.

Dr. Hornberg said everything was fine, she was doing very well. They still couldn't choose two baby's names.

One day Israel came home and blurted out, "Julia, I've been thinking... if a boy, I like Maynard. There's a guy in the orchestra, you know him Maynard Fineman, the sax player... I just keep thinking to myself, how classy that name Maynard is... What do you think?"

"Well, I never thought of that one... let's think about it, we still have about ten days," replied Julia.

The next morning, November 11, Julia was rushed to the hospital with labor pains. At 1:15 PM she had a

7.15 pound baby boy. The hospital did not yet have a given name. The birth certificate was filled out with the name of 'Baby Boy Turow.'

President Herbert Hoover was working for a month, maybe the economy would get a little better, anything at all would be a little help. A lot of people were still out of work, still long lines for work and food.

Juilliard School of Music in New York was moving along pretty much as normal. The finest school in the world for the arts will always attract talented students. However, for the moment, Professor Marvin Silverman and Maestro Eric Galliano had to find a reason to bring Israel Turow back to help in some capacity. The teachers had a long range plan for Israel and Israel knew nothing about it. The teachers were going to have to come up with some kind of a story.

After dinner one evening, a long distance call came in from New York. Israel was nervous thinking something was wrong with his sister Sophie. Israel was relieved to find out the call was from his friend and former Juilliard teacher, Marvin Silverman. After exchanging some pleasantries, Israel asked, "So what's up Professor Silverman?"

The teacher answered, "Israel, we've known each other long enough to call each other by our first names. Please call me Marvin."

"Okay, Marvin, what's up?"

Silverman and Maestro had decided on the following story: "Everything is going well at school, except we're a little short in one area. We need a former teacher or student who can come in and help out, around the first of the month. He can come in a few days or a whole week if he's got the time," explained the teacher.

Israel's reply, "Why not just hire a new teacher?"

"That's the problem," Marvin answered, "we don't need a full time teacher, we just need someone around the first of each month, for a day or two. Someone like you, who can step right in and help out in different areas... someone we don't have to teach what to do. Who can jump right in, like you!"

Israel was stunned and hesitated. "I don't know... I've got the time... not working for the moment. But now I have a little boy and..."

"Izzy, hold on, I know you have to discuss it with Julia, but here's my thought... come up to New York for a day. Maestro, you, and I will go over the whole picture, money and everything. I'll put a ticket in the mail today. You've got nothing to lose!" Israel said, "Okay, I'll call the day before I come."

"Great," Marvin answered, "by the way, be sure you

bring your violin!"

CHAPTER 40

Israel and Julia talked it over. What was to lose? Go to New York on the first of the month, come home in a day or two. Israel knew the routine, knew what had to be done first of the month. Jump in and out of violin and conductor's classes as needed, help with scheduling, always have a place to eat and sleep, either at school or with sister Sophie. And they sent a whole book of train tickets, no problem! He just didn't quite understand why Maestro and Marvin Silverman wanted him to play the violin for them an hour or two before he left each time. Like he was being graded or something. If they just liked to hear him play, so be it! The extra money each month can't hurt either. Running the orchestra weekend dates, doing dozens of other things, plus running to New York every month could get a little tiring.

One night after drying off from a bath, Israel noticed a little lump behind his left collarbone. He was sure it was from the placement of the violin because that's exactly where it rested. Israel decided to use a double shoulder pad when playing the violin. Hopefully, that would take care of the problem, plus he'd keep his eye on it.

After a month or so, Israel noticed the lump had not gone away, in fact, it had gotten slightly larger. Julia insisted Israel call Dr. Hornberg for an appointment. After a physical from the doctor, the report showed a very low grade fever and a tiny loss of weight. Dr. Hornberg wanted Israel to make an appointment with Dr. Greenberg, a specialist at Johns Hopkins Hospital. Dr. Hornberg told Israel and Julia, "It could be absolutely nothing, but I'd rather be sure."

Two weeks after the biopsy, Dr. Greenberg's office called and asked Israel to make an appointment for consultation. Dr. Greenberg explained, "Israel, you have Hodgkin's Disease. The good thing is we caught it early!"

Hodgkin's Disease, or Hodgkin's Lymphoma, is a cancer of the lymphatic system, which is part of the immune system. Cells in the lymphatic system grow abnormally and may spread into other parts of the body, making it difficult for the body to fight infection. The lymphatic system includes the lymph nodes, the spleen, the thymus gland, and bone marrow. Lymphoma can occur in any of these parts of the body, as well as other areas. Lymphoma originates in white blood cells called lymphocytes. The symptoms of Hodgkin's Disease include lymph node swelling in the areas of the neck, armpits, or groin, without pain, fever or chills, night sweats, unexplained weight loss, decrease in appetite, and skin itching. Although it is not known exactly why people develop the disease, those who are older or have weakened immune systems are at elevated risk. Some people will not need treatment right away. In cases in which the cancer is slow moving, a physician may opt to monitor the condition regularly until treatment is needed. Treatment for the disease usually will involve radiation or stem cell transplantation.

Dr. Greenberg continued, "For the moment, we'll do nothing. If you feel tired, rest for an hour or two. Try to drink three milkshakes a week with two raw eggs in them. It'll give you a little extra stamina. See you in three months, unless you need me."

CHAPTER 41

When working at the Valencia Theatre, Israel and Julia were able to put some money away. Fortunately, it had been a big help during some hard times. But it wouldn't last unless Israel could find additional income over the orchestra Bar Mitzvah and Wedding money.

To find a full time job that would guarantee him weekends off would not be easy and with all his hard work, he certainly didn't want to give up his violin. The only thing that might make sense was to find a small business, where he could control his own hours and still make additional income. He didn't know where to start.

One night over dinner with Mama and Papa Benesh, Israel explained his plan. By coincidence, Papa told them he was thinking the same thing. He had already spoken to a business broker who'd found something very interesting.

Israel blurted out, "But Pa, how'd you know?"

The father quickly answered, "What do you think, I just *got off* the boat?"

They all screamed in hysterics. Harry Benesh was always one step ahead! The place had a lot of pluses and very few minuses. It was an established business, having been there over ten years on a good traffic corner on Barkley Street in the middle of town.

It carried canned goods, ice cream, candy, soft drinks, and coddies. (Yes! I said coddies!) And it had a beer and wine license. It included a corner, three story row house. In the front was the store, with a full basement, with living room and kitchen just behind. The second floor had two bedrooms and a full bath. The third floor had two bedrooms. Another big plus, one part of the second floor was a self-contained, separate apartment with a bedroom, full bath, living room, kitchen, and separate entrance. It had a tenant, a former registered nurse, who had been there for years and planned to stay forever.

She paid rent on the first of the month and was never a day late. Papa said the clincher was, "The owners take a modest weekly salary and still shows a profit at the end of the year. Also, they're older and want to retire. I think we can make a good deal."

Harry Benesh went to the bank to talk about the mortgage. It worked out, with the down payment he negotiated, the monthly payments were cheaper to buy than to rent. After forty five days, Israel, Papa, the broker, and the seller all met at the Settlement Company to close the transaction. The previous owner stayed a week after settlement to help in the transition. Israel and Julia had themselves a new business.

CHAPTER 42

For the first few months, Israel did not make it to New York. They understood, there was no problem. However, Israel did practice on the violin three times a week in the large basement. Just moving in and getting settled was a little hectic. But once everything was in place, things seemed to go a lot smoother.

The previous owner had specific days for each vendor. Storage of heavy items like soft drinks, beer and wine cases had to be stored in the basement. Conveniently, they came in through the side door of the building, allowing the vendor to eliminate coming through the store. He took his product directly down the steps to the basement storage. He also filled the store ice cooler to keep the bottles cold. The lighter items like candy, cakes, cookies, canned goods, milk, ice cream products, and cigarettes came in through the front door. The shelves or cases were filled as needed by the vendor. The only "open food" item was coddies (codfish cakes), which came in a covered container and were replaced every two days. It didn't take long for Israel and Julia to catch on. The most important thing was physically checking what you received before signing for it, and to be sure you got a copy. Sometimes the vendors had to wait a few minutes if the store was busy, but they understood. The vendors were extremely helpful and honest. They kind of ran the show in a helpful way and always kept the owners happy. If receiving was done correctly, when the monthly invoices came in, it was easy to match up to the receiving and pay the bill.

Two perks Israel and Julia had no advanced knowledge of, came as a pleasant surprise. On the corner, just in front of the store was a police call box. This was where the officer on duty called in every few hours. Times were varied for general protection. Often, there were two. This meant, most of the time, there were police around the area. This was very comforting, especially, in the evening when it got dark. Officers Todd and Bluey, who worked the night shift, generally stuck their heads in the door at closing, which was nine PM, just to say good night.

The other pleasant surprise were the neighbors Ron and Betty White, who lived two doors away.

They were in the store so much, they became part time helpers. Whenever the store was busy, if they were around, they automatically helped customers. They had certain hours where they actually were on the payroll, like Sundays at twelve PM, when many customers were coming from church. The Whites had worked for the previous owners for several years and even had a key to the store. When offering to return it, Israel told Ron to keep it.

Israel and Julia were thrilled to meet Ron and Betty and soon became friends. Occasionally, they even had dinner together. Ron was a retired mailman, honest as the day is long. They had no children. Ron was also great at fixing things, he was a perfect handyman. After six months, Israel and Julia were happy with the way things were going. They took a modest weekly salary and after paying the monthly bills, they still had some money in the bank. That was a good sign.

There was only one problem. There was a three year old little boy running around and he now knew where the candy and cookie cases were. Worse than that, he just found out how the sliding glass doors opened!

CHAPTER 43

It was the first night of Passover. That meant the big Seder at Papa Benesh's house. Rhey and Bibi were married to Sol and Luki but had no children yet. There were certain rules when you had dinner at the Benesh's, especially Passover! There was the elaborate table with all the trimmings and Papa Benesh leading a very intense, full Seder. No one says a word unless you're called upon. And, nobody is ever late! At the table was Leonard Benesh, who was in high school, so there was no reason to be late. Also, there was Sol and Luki with their wives. Both men were appliance reps on the road, so their time was their own, and there was no reason to be late. There was Mama Leah and Papa Benesh and lastly, there was Julia and her three year old son, Maynard.

There was an empty chair next to Julia being saved for her husband, Israel. It was previously explained to Papa that Israel would be a little late because he had to close the store. Papa waited as long as possible but had to get started with the Seder. As Papa was reading and chanting the service and occasionally looking out at his guests, you could see he was steaming! After about half way through the service, the dining room door quietly opened and in slipped Israel. He quietly moved around the table to kiss each lady on the check, kiss his wife and son and sits down. Not a word was spoken. In his heart, Harry Benesh felt for what Israel was going through. He had a special respect and love for this son-in-law, knowing how hard he was working, while carrying a serious disease.

Papa puts down his book and told everyone to take a sip of wine. He looked at Israel and said, "Israel, suppose you tell us all a short version of the story of Passover!"

Israel knew by the tone of his voice and smile on his face, that Papa was not mad. Everyone in the room felt a little more relaxed. And Israel started. "The Jews were slaves in Egypt under Pharaoh. Moses tried many times asking Pharaoh to 'let our people go!' But he would not. One day, Moses had an idea. He packed special food to give to Pharaoh to taste. So, he went to Pharaoh and said, 'Your Highness'—"

Papa Benesh blurted out, "Israel, Moses called Pharaoh 'Your Highness'?"

Israel replied, "What's he going to call him, Meyer?"

Everyone broke up! Papa had to turn his face away to shield his laughter. After the room settled down,

Israel continued, 'Pharaoh, I brought you a gift, something to eat, here, taste this.' Pharaoh eats and says, 'Moses, this is delicious, what is it?' 'It is a coddie, Your Highness!' Everyone breaks up! 'And where does one find this delicious delicacy?' Pharaoh asked. Moses replies, 'At Turow's Confectionary on Barclay Street!' —"

The room is in hysterics. Even Papa couldn't stop laughing. He yelled, "The Seder is over... let's eat!"

When the room settled down to normal conversations, everyone noticed that the little three year old was still laughing and wouldn't stop. Julia asked, "Honey, what is it, what are you laughing at?"

Finally, still giggling, little Maynard blurted out, "Daddy called Pharaoh Meyer!"

CHAPTER 44

The Bar Mitzvah and wedding orchestra business was unsteady. On Saturdays the affair had to be after eight PM and Sundays late afternoon or evenings. These were the times the store was closed or close to closing.

Between Israel, Julia, Ron, and Betty (plus the second floor tenant/nurse) the store was pretty well covered. When there were no weekend affairs booked, the orchestra met Sunday mornings at eleven AM for rehearsals. Israel had a large basement under the store, where the musicians brought their own folding chairs and music stands. All the players had regular weekday jobs, so meeting Sunday mornings was no problem. The musicians were eager to rehearse because the Bar Mitzvah/wedding money was a nice plus. With Israel practicing almost every night on his own, when Sunday rehearsals came along, he was pretty sharp. Running both the orchestra business and the store, in a few months, things started to fall into place.

The previous owner told Israel that the empty store across the street had been vacant for over a year. Israel and Julia didn't pay too much attention to it. One day, out of the blue, there were big signs all over the front windows, "Grand Opening! Big Discounts!" Small crowds were going in and out. It was obvious, the Turow's were losing business. Israel had Ron check it out. Ron came back with a full report. The new store carried pretty much the same type of merchandise: canned goods, candies, sodas, ice cream, etc. In some cases the brand names were different, like Pepsi instead of Coke. However, Ron pointed out, the big difference was everything was priced two to five cents lower.

Israel quickly set in motion a few changes. "Meet the price if asked," he ordered. He also made some signs with "in store specials" on certain days.

"Most important," Israel reminded everyone, "they don't have a beer and wine license!" At least not yet.

Another important thing Israel did, he told every vendor he bought from, "If you sell him, I'm looking elsewhere!" Most of the vendors got the message and acted accordingly. In the big picture, it set the tone. But, every day, Israel kept thinking of ways to improve the store's business. One day, it hit him.

"In the next few weeks it'll be Spring. Generally, nice weather for the next six months. Since many of the customers come home from church between eleven and noon, why not have orchestra rehearsal outside, along the side of the building, at the same time? If it rains, we cancel!" Israel asked the musicians their opinion. They loved the idea. "What do we have to lose?"

Israel asked Officers Todd and Bluey if there were any problems or restrictions using the side pavement to practice? "No," they said, "as long as you don't block automobile or pedestrian traffic." Todd added, "We can help you with that."

At first, there was a small crowd. The next time the crowd was larger and by the third week, people crowded the area with folding chairs, starting at ten AM. It was working.

When the music ended at noon, the store was opened and it was packed! Sundays became a big day and it carried over into the week. People came in just to ask, "Is there music this Sunday?" And while they were in, generally they picked up something. Business kept getting better. While all this was going on, nobody was paying much attention to the store across the street. One day they saw a big sign on the front window,

"Closed!"

CHAPTER 45

There were occasional days Israel felt tired in the late afternoon and he would go up on the sofa and lie down for an hour or two. There were other days when he was full of energy and was unstoppable from morning until bedtime. However, lately, he seemed to be resting more than usual and his appetite was a little off. He felt a little weaker some days. After discussing it, Israel and Julia decided to call Dr. Homberg for a house visit, not an emergency, just a checkup.

After Dr. Hornberg completed his examination, he asked Israel, "How are you sleeping?"

"Not good Doc, sometimes I wake up and can't go back to sleep," replied Israel.

"I think that's one of the reasons for being tired, you're not getting enough sleep. Here, take one of these before bedtime. It'll help you sleep! Also, remember, you're taking on quite a lot. You've got violin, you've got orchestra, occasional traveling to New York plus, you've got the store! You're carrying quite a load!"

After a pause, Israel asked the question he'd been

holding in. "Well, Doc, what did you find, what's going on?"

The doctor answered, "Israel, I don't have any bad news. There's been no big change since the last time I examined you."

Israel sat back, somewhat relaxed. The doctor continued, "But there are some ongoing issues we already know about. There's no emergency... when you get time, I would like you to go back to see Dr. Greenberg, at Hopkins. See what he thinks about the overall picture. He might want to start some treatment that will make you feel stronger."

The pills did help Israel sleep. He wasn't taking the afternoon nap as often. Actually, he was feeling a lot better. He even added back his New York visits. Often on the hot nights in the middle of the summer, Israel and Julia would bring out their canvas and wood sling chairs and sit out in front of the store to catch a cool breeze. When a customer went in, one would get up and take care of business. Maynard would be playing somewhere in the area and could hear the call when it was bedtime.

One evening, about eight PM, Julia yelled out, "Maynard, it's eight o'clock, time to get ready for bed!"

A minute or two later, the boy showed up, a little

sweaty, saying, "I'm here Mom!"

"It's time to wash up, say your prayers and go to bed, and don't forget to brush your teeth!" said Julia.

"Okay, goodnight Mom, goodnight Dad," Maynard said as he kissed them.

As the boy walked away, Israel said, "Come here, Son, I want you to do me a favor." Israel put his arm around his boy and said, "When you say your prayers tonight, will you ask God to make your Daddy better... to make the sickness go away?"

Maynard kissed his father again and said, "Okay Daddy!"

The six year old went up to his room, washed his hands and face, and brushed his teeth. He knelt down next to his bed, folded his hands and started to speak. "Now I lay me down to sleep, I pray to God my soul to keep, if I should die before I wake, I pray to God my soul to take. God bless Mommy and God bless Daddy. Dear God, please make Daddy better. Please make him not be sick any more. Please make him strong again, so he can play with me like he used to."

CHAPTER 46

One of Israel's favorite mornings is Sunday. The store doesn't open until noon and orchestra practice isn't until eleven. He can sleep a little later and make his special breakfast; eggs, onions with salami, and other selective leftovers in the ice box. As he stood there stirring his concoction, Julia said, "Israel, how can you eat that in the morning, and the smell must drive Mrs. Levan, upstairs, crazy!"

"Honey, here try some, you'll love it!" he offered.

She yelled, "Get that stuff away from me!"

"Honey, do you know this dish puts lead in my pencil?" he said, as he sat down munching on a bagel.

"Speaking of your pencil, I've got some news for you!" she said. Emptying the frying pan onto his plate, he didn't hear everything she said, but heard "your pencil" and thought that was funny!

"What did you say about my pencil?" he asks.

Julia replied, "I think your pencil has been working overtime... I'm pregnant!"

Israel put the bagel down, saying, "Honey, are you sure, I mean, why didn't you say something, when did it happen? I mean..." He got up and kissed her.

She laughed at all the silly questions. She replied, "Yes, I'm sure. It's due late November-December."

"Great, sweetheart, how are you feeling?" he said, as he kissed her again. She told him she was doing fine, and she would just have to slow down a bit as we get closer.

"Absolutely, I'll be bringing in Ron more, so you just slow down whenever you have to," answered Israel.

Julia puts her hand on Israel's and said, "Honey, just one favor, please... no more waiting until the last minute to come up with a name. This time, we'll have two names ready, okay?"

"Absolutely," answered Israel. "One thing I know right now, for sure, if it's a boy, I'm not calling him Meyer!"

A week later, Israel brought nurse/tenant Claudia Levan up to date. They discussed payment or rent credit and she was thrilled to help anytime needed. She was familiar with the third floor nursery room that Maynard used when he was a baby. The boy moved down to the second floor bedroom a couple of years ago when he changed to his big bed. It was great having Mrs. Levan living in the same building. It was like having their own full time nurse, available all the time!.

Israel and Ron agreed on the arrangements. Ron and wife Betty would each work into a gradual full time schedule as Julia cut back on her hours. Also, Israel and Ron worked out a commission arrangement against his hourly pay. Ron was thrilled. Hopefully, things were falling into place.

One afternoon, when Maynard was eating an ice cream cone, Israel hugged his son and said, "Maynard, time is flying... you're getting to be a big boy... before you know it, we'll be talking about your Bar Mitzvah! Tomorrow, let's walk across the street to the little Hebrew School and speak to Mr. Spegal about starting Hebrew School!"

The boy asked, "When do I go Dad... I've got regular school all week!"

"You'll go after school... it's only a few hours a week. We'll check tomorrow and see what Mr. Spegal says," answered Israel.

"Okay, Dad," the boy replied.

Israel and his son climbed the thin wooden steps leading from the synagogue, to the second floor. There were several small groups of boys working together. They were divided by their general age groups. The teacher moved from group to group, spending approximately fifteen minutes with each group. The man approached Israel with his hand extended, saying, "Hello, I'm Max Spegal!"

"Hello," Israel answered. "This is my boy Maynard. He's six and I think he should start Hebrew School, what do you think, Mr. Spegal?"

"I know who you are, I've stopped in your store often. Yes, six is a perfect age... he'll start with the youngest group over here. First, let's talk about Hebrew Name. You said his name is Maynard? His Hebrew name is Mayer! Here, take this information form, it'll answer all your questions. For now, he'll come Tuesdays and Thursdays three to five, if those hours are convenient for you. As he gets older, we'll increase it a bit, to get ready for Bar Mitzvah. Now, leave him with me, I'll have one of the older boys bring him home, when he's done today." Israel kissed his son and left.

The teacher said to the boy, "Mayer, watch my mouth and say what I say... BAA, BAW, BEW!"

CHAPTER 47

Israel was working a hectic schedule. He knew it, but generally he had been feeling pretty good and didn't pay too much attention to it. One day, he noticed he was getting very tired late in the day. He lied down for a bit and tried to rest. He noticed his tiredness coming more often and knew now it was not normal. He did not want to upset Julia, she had enough to worry about. On his own, he made an appointment with Dr. Greenberg at Hopkins. He spoke to the doctor, explained how he was feeling. The doctor did his examination. When it was completed, the doctor and Israel met in the office for consultation. Naturally, Israel was concerned but hoped for the best.

The doctor started by saying, "Israel, the good news is, I don't have any bad news. Meaning, the lymphoma is still present in the body and is being fought by the white blood cells. The stronger the white blood cells are, the better fight they put up. Right now, there's not much change since last time. However, we don't know what might happen a few months from now. If the white cells break down, the cancer could spread. Maybe we can give the white cells some help. A few years back, medical scientists discovered Radium Dichloride, which is a radioactive drug that behaves in a similar way to calcium and collects in cancer cells that have spread to the bones and other areas. The radioactive particles in Radium can kill the tumor cells and reduce the pain they can cause. The Radium treatment is given in very small doses because it is radioactive. Treatment is about thirty minutes, plus a thirty minute rest period. There have been cases where the Radium treatments have completely removed the tumorous cells. Israel, I think we should give it a try!"

One night after the kids went to bed and Julia seemed in a joyful mood, very casually, Israel told his wife the whole story. He was careful to emphasize all of the pluses and not dwell on the negatives. Julia cried, Israel held her tightly. They talked for hours. They decided Israel would go for Radium Treatments.

Israel had two treatments over a four week period. After a small setback of weakness and nauseousness, Israel quickly recovered. He felt like his old self. He was hoping for the best. After all, he had to get ready for the new baby.

CHAPTER 48

They say, generally, delivery of the second child is much easier on the mother. That definitely was the case with Julia. She had normal pains and easily delivered a seven pound baby girl on December 3, 1936, at 3:36 PM. Her name was Ellen Joan. The ironic thing was this little princess's features were absolutely perfect. There were no wrinkles, no folds, no creases, only a perfect little face, like she was carved out of stone. There was a tiny little nose, tiny little mouth, perfect little eyebrows, beautiful eyes, and skin like a Hollywood model. Thank God, she came out perfect. The nurses and Julia were thrilled with her overall appearance.

Israel was like a little boy in a candy shop. He couldn't keep his hands off her. Every time you looked around, Israel was carrying his little girl. Having a boy was wonderful, but there was nothing like having a little girl.

When bringing her home, Israel was carrying her. When turning the baby over to the nurse, Mrs. Levan, she quickly put the baby to bed in the nursery. Israel was the last one to leave the nursery. Julia went into the bedroom to rest. While little Ellen was sleeping, Israel would peek in on her several times. Sometimes, when the baby was being changed or fed, Mrs. Levan, in a friendly manner, would have to shoo Israel out of the room, because he was in the way.

One day, when Bibi and Loki were visiting, Bibi snuck up to the nursery, unknown to anybody while the baby napped. When Israel found out, he ran up to the nursery, quietly opened the door and gave Bibi a signal to get out.

When out of the room, he explained, "No one goes into that room without the nurse, him, or Julia. Nobody!"

Bibi acknowledged and went downstairs. Israel took a peek in. Israel guarded that nursery door like a marine on guard duty. Nothing was going to harm his precious El-Jay!

One day, a few months later, on a quiet afternoon, Israel snuck up, put the baby in a bassinet and brought her down to the store with him. He put the bassinet behind the cash register, where he could play and talk to her. He also would show certain customers that he knew, his new baby daughter.

After a few minutes, he could hear Julia screaming, "Where's the baby?" He yelled back, "The baby is with me in the store!" Julia ran down hysterical, "Are you out of your mind?"

Sheepishly, Israel said, "I just wanted to spend some time with her!"

Julia grabbed the baby and went upstairs.

They didn't talk for the rest of the day.

CHAPTER 49

Maynard was now six years old. After baby Ellen was born, it seemed like Israel spent less time with his son, not on purpose, it just seemed that way. But Maynard was not a baby anymore. Maybe he was too big to be carried? The boy wondered if his daddy still loved him. Could Mommy and Daddy love two kids at the same time?

When Julia gave her son a bath, it was wash, dry, brush teeth, pajamas, then bed. When Daddy gave him a bath, there was time to play. Often, Israel would make little sails from toilet paper, attach them to the soap and make little boats that they both would play with. When Daddy dried his son, he would tickle the boy under his arms and both would be laughing. That was fun.

Some days Israel would stand in front of the mirror, with scissors. Maynard asked, "What are you doing?"

Israel answered, "Trimming my mustache."

Daddy sometimes wore the mustache and other times he did not.

Aunt Bibi always said, "When Israel wears the

mustache, he looks like Errol Flynn the movie star!"

Errol Flynn was a pretty handsome guy, that was quite a compliment!

One Saturday there was a heavy snow. By Sunday, the snow had stopped and the sun came out. Everyone was shoveling or playing in the snow.

Daddy bundled Maynard up in a coat, gloves, hat, and galoshes. Israel had on a brown wool coat with big brown buttons, dark brown cloth work gloves, like he sold in the store, and rubbers over his shoes. Israel told Julia and Ron that he was taking Maynard sleigh riding in the street in front of the store.

Daddy tied a rope to the front wooden handles of the sled and carried it to the gutter area of the street. Israel sat his son squarely on the sled and showed him how to hold on. The boy was a little nervous but tried to be brave.

Israel pulled the sled slowly and they moved up the street. The little boy hung on! When they came to the end of the street, Israel turned the sled around and they went the other way. It was fun. It was just the little boy and his Daddy, playing together!

After a few times, Israel started to slowly run, moving the sled faster. One time, when running pretty fast, the sled hit something and turned over. The boy fell off and started to cry.

Israel quickly picked up his son, brushed him off and asked, "You okay, big boy?"

Israel held the boy tightly and gave him a kiss on the cheek.

The little boy squeezed his Daddy tightly and kissed him back, thinking, 'my Daddy must still love me!'

CHAPTER 50

The invitation read: You Are Invited! The Garfield Clothing Company wishes to honor Harry Hyman Benesh with a Testimonial Dinner, celebrating his thirty years of service, dedication, and loyalty. Place: Belvedere Hotel, Date: April 15, 1937, Time: Cocktails: 6:30 PM, Dinner: 7:30 PM, Dress: Black Tie.

The family was excited, what a great honor! Papa Benesh called Julia a week before, offered to drive, he would pick them up at six PM. Coincidentally, the date of the affair was the same date as Julia and Israel's tenth anniversary. It didn't matter though, they were happy for Papa and they would celebrate another night. The doorman greeted them and took the car. As they crossed the lobby, it seemed like a quiet night, only a few people sitting around. They walked down the hall to the main ballroom.

They opened the door, must be the wrong place, pitch black and quiet. As they turned to exit, the lights went on, everyone yelled "SURPRISE!" The orchestra played, 'Hail, Hail, the Gangs All Here!' A large sign across the room said "Happy Anniversary!" Confetti was flying everywhere!

Julia and Israel were totally shocked. Julia asked, "Papa, what about your Testimonial Dinner?"

Papa yelled back, "Oh, that was last month!"

They all laughed, hugged, and mixed with everyone. It was unbelievable who was there, both families, all the gang from the old neighborhood, guys and girls, teachers from several schools, the whole orchestra (led by Arnold Hartman) and even Marvin Silverman and Maestro Eric Galliano from New York! One hell of an affair!

After a few drinks and mixing with the crowd, everyone was seated. Arnold added greetings and read some congratulatory telegrams. After a few minutes, Arnold brought Maestro to the microphone. After well-wishes, the Maestro spoke, "Julia, in honor of your tenth anniversary, I have for you a front row seat to Carnegie Hall for October 15, 1937, where they will be celebrating the Octoberfest, featuring the New York Symphony Orchestra!"

An applause was heard.

Maestro moved from the mic, a few seconds passed, finally, Israel yelled, "Maestro, thank you... but you know, it's my anniversary too, wouldn't you think I'd like to be there too?"

Maestro moved to the mic and answered, "Oh yes, young man, you'll be there... you'll definitely be there."

With that, Maestro pulled a folded paper out of his jacket packet, continued to unfold and read from a large flier. "Carnegie Hall announces its Octoberfest, Saturday October 15, 1937, featuring the New York Symphony Orchestra, led by Maestro Eric Galliano and guest Soloist Israel Stanly Turow!" The crowd screamed.

Israel screamed, "What... what did you say?"

Arnie Hartman answered over the mic, "That's right Izzy, you're playing the Big Hall!"

"If I'm dreaming, please don't wake me up... Maestro, Arnie, what's going on?" yelled Israel.

Maestro answered, "Israel, Arnold and I have been working on the contract and the details for a few weeks. He'll be able to answer all your questions." Arnold went to Israel and embraced as life-long friends.

"A far cry from the ship's Talent Contest, huh, Izzy?" Arnold went to the mic. "Israel, Julia, there's a few other goodies I want to tell you about. The following already has been taken care of," started

Arnold, "so there's not much you can do about it! Rehearsals for the concert start Monday October tenth. Julia and Israel will be the guests of the Waldorf Astoria Hotel from October tenth through the sixteenth. Parents Jenny and Izik Turow and Leah and Harry Benesh will be guests of the hotel, Friday October fourteenth through the sixteenth. Round trip transportation from Baltimore to New York will be provided. Also, several dozen tickets are being held for family and friends as needed."

Arnold continued, "Nurse Claudia Levan has been engaged to take care of the children and finally, Ron and Betty Smith have been engaged to run the store the week you are away. I believe that's it... any questions Izzy?"

By this time, Israel had had three glasses of champagne and was feeling pretty good. With a little humor he answered, "Well... well... what about my kid's Hebrew School?"

Everyone laughed and Arnie answered, "I guess he'll just have to go!"

CHAPTER 51

Julia called Ron and Betty to take care of the store Sunday. She was going to let Israel sleep late. Israel climbed out of bed about noon, ate a little breakfast and went back to bed. Like all hangovers after a big night, he felt kind of punk. He called Arnold Hartman to get some answers on a few items on his mind. One thing Israel questioned was the sheet music he was going to play at the concert.

Arnold explained, "Maestro is sending you all the music information, overnight mail Tuesday. He and I already discussed it."

Then Israel asked, "Arn, so I wasn't dreaming, all of that from last night was really true, huh?"

"You got it Izzy, you're playing the Big Hall October fifteenth!" answered Arnold.

"Okay, I've got plenty of work ahead," said Israel. "Please keep me informed on things every few weeks or so."

"Will do" answered Arnie.

They both hung up. Israel went back to bed.

After a good night's sleep, Israel woke up feeling pretty good. He got up at regular time, had breakfast and opened the store. He put in a full day, received some goods, took care of some customers and asked Julia to please have dinner ready at five. He wanted to go practice in the basement a few evenings a week. After receiving all the music and instructions from Maestro, he worked very diligently on his music almost every night.

Some days Israel would try to take a nap before dinner. It didn't always happen, it depended on how busy he was in the store. On the days he didn't take a nap, he was extremely tired the next day. He understood and did the best he could. Occasionally, after putting the children to bed, Julia would come down to the basement and listen to her husband.

She told him, and meant it, "You have never played better!" This was good to hear. He thought he was playing well, and hearing it from Julia, confirmed his feelings. Once a month, Israel would confer with Maestro over a piece of music. They kept in touch.

After several months at this pace, Israel started to tire easily. He also wasn't eating with the usual appetite and he had lost a couple of pounds. Julia kept pushing the milkshakes with eggs and other heavy protein foods. She now had some doubts about his general condition and would wait one more month before she really pushed for him to cancel. After several weeks, Julia called Arnold Hartman to bring him up to date. He told her he was coming right over to talk to Israel. Arnold arrived and did not like the way Israel looked. The three of them spoke and Julia and Arnold tried to convince Israel to cancel. With tears in his eyes, Israel pleaded his case, that he was feeling alright.

Saying nothing to Julia and Arnold, he had a gut feeling that this may be his last concert. He didn't want to lose the opportunity. He had to go through with it. After a lengthy discussion, they agreed to go forward with certain conditions: Arnold would take Israel to rehearsals, stay during rehearsals, and bring him back to the hotel. Also, nothing was to be said to Maestro or Marvin Silverman unless it came from Israel. October ninth, Israel, Julia, and Arnold headed for New York. Rehearsals started tomorrow. At the first rehearsal, Maestro made introductions, set the ground rules and went to work.

When practicing at home, Israel had pushed very hard and it showed at the rehearsal. He played beautifully and was very confident. Each day, the orchestra and Israel blended closer together. Maestro was very pleased.

Some days Israel would sit after a portion was played then stand for the next portion. Nobody paid much attention to it, but Arnold was concerned. The week flew by and everyone was ready. Maestro gave everyone Friday off, the day before the concert. The entire company was instructed to eat a light meal beforehand on Saturday and be at the Big Hall by 6:30 PM for a quick run-through before the eight PM concert. Israel was very happy with the day off, he needed a little rest, he was weak and tired. With the extra rest, he guessed he would be fine. Israel had a sleepless night and Saturday morning he was completely rung out. Julia was watching him but he said nothing. He just tried to go through the motions like everything was fine.

But it wasn't. He was running a slight fever and was extremely weak.

CHAPTER 52

Julia called Arnold and told him, "Israel is sick, he can't go on, we must cancel!" Arnold came right over. He took one look at Israel and knew there was a problem. Israel sat them both down and spoke from the heart.

"I know I've had better days and I'm not feeling great, but with your help, I'll make it, I know I will!"

Arnold responded, "Izzy, if we call Maestro right now, he can get Marvin Silverman to take over, and we can get you to the hospital... you need care, right now!"

"If I miss this chance, it won't come again, I know it's today or never," Israel pleaded. "Here's my suggestion: I eat this whole breakfast, drink plenty of water, go take a shower, and get back in bed. It's now ten AM... if I'm not better by two, we'll cancel. Please give me this one chance, please!"

Arnold looked at Julia saying, "It really won't make any difference to Marvin, he knows the music, he's been playing it all his life... let's give it a try, Jul. I'll call you at two. If the fever's gone and he's feeling stronger, it's a go, if not, we cancel. Agreed Israel?"

"Agreed, Arnie," Israel answered.

As Arnold hugged Julia and left, Israel was eating his breakfast. After breakfast, Israel showered and got back in bed. He was drinking plenty of water. He started to read the *New York Times*, and there was a writeup about tonight's concert. After a few minutes, Israel falls asleep. Julia could hear a slight snore, which was a good sign, it meant he was sleeping soundly. Julia felt better.

At just past one, Israel opened his eyes and said, "How's my best girl?" Julia ran to him and felt his head. He felt much cooler, probably normal.

She kissed him and asked, "How do you feel?"

"Much better, sweetheart," he replied. He even looked better. At two, Arnold called and Julia gave him the update.

"Great!" bellowed Arnold, "we have to meet the limousine at six, I'll pick him up at 5:45!"

"He'll be ready" answered Julia. For the next few hours Israel and Julia spoke about many things. Before long it was five o'clock and Israel has to get dressed. He gobbled down a piece of toast with jelly and finished a cup of tea. Then he started getting dressed. He started with socks, shoes, pants, and shirt. Israel wrestled with his bowtie. He got a little help from his wife. He put on his jacket and looked in the mirror, and said, "Not too bad, huh Jul?"

She remarked how handsome he looked. Just then, the doorbell rang, it was Arnold.

"Well, who is this guy? Quite a difference since this morning!" he said.

"Yea, feeling much better, too!" answered Israel.

Arnold confirmed, "Julia, you're coming with your parents later, right?" "Yes," she replied.

Israel and Julia embraced, whispered something in each other's ears, and kissed. Arnold and Israel took off.

The orchestra, Maestro, Israel, and Arnold are all waiting behind the curtain in the green room. Maestro wondered why Arnold was there, but no problem, maybe something Israel requested? At 7:50, it was announced, the orchestra filed out and entered onto the stage to a rousing ovation. Maestro followed with a repeat ovation. Lastly, Israel Turow started to walk out and stopped.

Quickly, Arnold Hartman came to Israel, put his arm around Israel's back and together, both walked towards the podium. When reaching the chair next to the podium, Israel sat down. The applause, which never stopped, now reached its highest pitch as the audience sensed there was some sort of an issue with Israel Turow.

When things quieted down, Maestro lifted his baton in the ready position. Israel tried as hard as he could to stand. The Overture started. As the orchestra continued into the opening aria, it was time for Israel to join in. He came in perfectly and continued playing beautifully. Maestro, and the entire orchestra, noticed something different. For the first time in the twenty years Maestro had known Israel, he never saw him perform sitting down! Maestro knew something was wrong.

Without anyone noticing, he gave a head nod to Marvin Silverman, his first violinist, to be prepared if there was a problem with Israel. Silverman acknowledged and everyone continued as normal. But, there was no problem, Israel was playing as well as he ever had.

The orchestra played and Israel played. It continued until everyone came to a lavish outro. A roaring applause followed. Maestro took his bow. He then signaled and the orchestra took their bow. He then looked at Israel, who did not get up. He smiled and nodded his head several times to acknowledge the applause.

Finally, with the help of Marvin Silverman, Israel

stood and started to walk stage right. After a few steps, Arnold Hartman appeared to take Israel from Silverman. Arnold and Israel slowly continued walking stage right.

Just before entering the wings, Israel stopped, faced the audience, smiled and nodded his head. He couldn't lift his arms as he was accustomed to. He wanted to thank them one more time. He and Arnold then turned and continued walking.

CHAPTER 53

The concert was over. But Israel was spent. He could hardly walk or even speak. Israel was also running a fever. He was rushed to New York General, a west-side hospital where he received intravenous dozes and several other medications. His doctor at Johns Hopkins Hospital in Baltimore was called and preparations were made for Israel to be transported first thing in the morning to Baltimore.

After several days of radiation and other treatment, Israel was resting comfortably. He spoke about the concert and asked Julia several times how it went. She said, "magnificent, as always." He whispered back, "I think it was my last one."

"Don't be silly dear, you're going to have many more," she answered, but he knew differently, even though it brought a smile to his face.

After a couple days, Israel was starting to feel a little stronger. Occasionally, he moved from the bed to the nearby chair. A day later, he was able to walk to the balcony to see his son, Maynard. The next day, Julia left the hospital at eight PM, feeling somewhat relieved.

Israel was in good spirits and seemed to be getting stronger. She was hoping for the best.

After falling into a deep sleep, at two AM, the cracking sound of the phone startled her. It was the hospital nurse. She tried to explain; after falling asleep, Israel woke up screaming, then fell into a coma. The doctor came quickly. He believed the Lymphoma from the dreaded Hodgkin's Disease had reached the brain. He thought it best to return to the hospital as quickly as possible.

Julia called Grandpa Benesh who immediately rushed over. Maynard's room was just across the hall. He woke up hearing his mom crying and saying, "Papa, what could have happened?"

Grandpa answered, "Hurry Julia, get dressed. We'll get all the answers when we get there."

In a few minutes, his Mom came into his room, leaned over, kissed him and said she would be back soon. "If you or the baby need anything, call Mrs. Levan." Baby Ellen's room was upstairs. She was still sleeping.

Maynard said, "Bye bye Mommy, please come back soon!"

One day later, October 23, 1937, Israel Turow

passed away. He was thirty-two years old . He never awoke from the coma.

He left a young widow of twenty-nine, a son seven years old and an infant daughter ten months old. Israel Stanley Turow, the Violin Virtuoso, had so much to give and so little time to give it.

He was laid to rest in a small cemetery in Baltimore, Maryland. The gravestone, selected by Grandpa Benesh, was nestled next to a clinging spruce tree whose branches guard the grave-site like a sentinel in the night. The tombstone was the shape of a tree trunk cut in half.

As Grandpa said, "A tree trunk cut in half--a lifetime cut in half!"

As the coffin was slowly lowered gently into the ground, Maynard stood by somewhat bewildered. He was only seven years old but knew the person he loved and called Daddy, his hero and best friend, was gone forever. He didn't realize at the time how much he would miss his father throughout his lifetime.

Now me, lay me, down to sleep, I pray the Lord my soul to keep, If I should die before I wake,

I pray the Lord my soul to take,

God bless Mommy and God Bless Daddy...........

Israel Stanley Turow – age 25

ORDER NO. [____]

NOV [____]

HEALTH DEPARTMENT—CITY OF BALTIMORE

CERTIFICATE OF BIRTH

D5882[_]

(1) PLACE OF BIRTH

CITY OF BALTIMORE

Registered No. [____]

(2) FULL NAME OF CHILD _____

(3) Sex of Child	(4) Twin, triplet, or other?	(5) Number in order of birth	(6) Legitimate	(7) Date of Birth [Month] [Day] [Year]

FATHER

MOTHER

(8) FULL NAME _____

(9) FULL MAIDEN NAME _____

(10) RESIDENCE _____

(11) RESIDENCE _____

(12) COLOR _____ (13) AGE AT LAST BIRTHDAY _____

(14) COLOR _____ (15) AGE AT LAST BIRTHDAY _____

(16) BIRTHPLACE _____

(17) BIRTHPLACE _____ Baltimore Md.

(18) OCCUPATION _____

(19) OCCUPATION Housewife

(20) Number of children born to this mother, including present birth _____

(21) Number of children of this mother now living _____

CERTIFICATE OF ATTENDING PHYSICIAN

(When there was no attending physician or midwife then the father, householder, etc., should make this return.)

(22) I hereby certify that I attended the birth of this child, who was _____ on the date above stated.

(A stillbirth requires a birth certificate and a death certificate which should be placed together. A stillborn child is one that does not breathe after birth.)

(23) Given name added from a supplemental report.

(24) Signature of Physician _____ Wm. B. Shapiro M.D.

Address 2415 Eutaw Place

FEB 8 1924

Received [____]

THIS IS TO CERTIFY THAT THE ABOVE IS A TRUE COPY OF A CERTIFICATE ON FILE IN THE BALTIMORE CITY HEALTH DEPARTMENT, BALTIMORE, MARYLAND.

WARNING: DO NOT ACCEPT THIS TRANSCRIPT UNLESS THE OFFICIAL DEPARTMENTAL SEAL IS AFFIXED HEREON. PLEASE NOTE SEAL IS IN BLUE.

Sidney Horton
BUREAU OF VITAL RECORDS

Robert E. Farber, M.D.
COMMISSIONER OF HEALTH AND REGISTRAR

Loew's Valencia Theatre staff,●a 1926.

MAYNARD TUROW

Born and raised in Baltimore, MD
Moved to Silver Spring, MD 1960
Wife-Marlyn
Children-Jodi and Stuart
Grandchildren-Sandi, Gregory, Jamie, Michael
Greatgrand Children-Shay and Miles
Sister-Ellen Joan
Veteran-1949-1951 U. S Marine Corps
Served aboard Battleship Missouri

Marlyn Dearest,
Thank you,
for your help, encouragement, love & support

LVU, ALW

Made in the USA
Middletown, DE
06 September 2023